INTEGRATED APPROACH TO TRADE AND TRANSPORT FACILITATION

MEASURING READINESS FOR SUSTAINABLE, INCLUSIVE, AND RESILIENT TRADE

DECEMBER 2022

ADB

ASIAN DEVELOPMENT BANK

© 2022 Asian Development Bank
6 ADB Avenue, Mandaluyong City, 1550 Metro Manila, Philippines
Tel +63 2 8632 4444; Fax +63 2 8636 2444
www.adb.org

Some rights reserved. Published in 2022.

ISBN 978-92-9269-981-9 (print); 978-92-9269-982-6 (electronic); 978-92-9269-983-3 (ebook)
Publication Stock No. TCS220596-2
DOI: http://dx.doi.org/10.22617/TCS220596-2

The views expressed in this publication are those of the authors and do not necessarily reflect the views and policies of the Asian Development Bank (ADB) or its Board of Governors or the governments they represent.

ADB does not guarantee the accuracy of the data included in this publication and accepts no responsibility for any consequence of their use. The mention of specific companies or products of manufacturers does not imply that they are endorsed or recommended by ADB in preference to others of a similar nature that are not mentioned.

By making any designation of or reference to a particular territory or geographic area, or by using the term "country" in this publication, ADB does not intend to make any judgments as to the legal or other status of any territory or area.

Corrigenda to ADB publications may be found at http://www.adb.org/publications/corrigenda.

Notes:
In this publication, "$" refers to United States dollars.
ADB recognizes "Russia" as the Russian Federation.

On the cover: Images used of agreement (handshake), digitalization (cell phone and application use), goods (container), and transport (truck hauling container) are all taken from ADB's Photo Library.

Cover design by Josef Ilumin.

Contents

Tables, Figures, and Boxes

Figures

Boxes

Foreword

Trade facilitation—customs modernization, simplification and harmonization of trade procedures, and regulatory transparency—is a key policy tool to enhance the seamless flow of goods across borders. A major milestone was achieved when in 2013 members of the World Trade Organization completed negotiation of the Trade Facilitation Agreement, which went into effect in 2017. The Agreement established multilateral rules to address at-the-border challenges. More recently, many countries have prioritized use of technology for automated customs systems, electronic submission of trade documents, single window systems, and other measures to expedite the flow of goods.

While at-the-border policy initiatives to support trade facilitation are commendable, discussions can and should be more comprehensive, that is, expanded to beyond-the-border measures related to transport infrastructure and connectivity currently discussed at the national level or at separate international forums. The division of government activities by sectors and/or jurisdiction often results in poor coordination, and hence less effective policy outcomes.

The inter-sectoral agendas of trade facilitation and transport connectivity, thus, should be brought under an integrated governance system that supports national policies to promote trade and value chain development, and also takes a comprehensive and holistic approach to diagnostics, performance assessment, and management of supply chain connectivity and logistics. After all, it is the combination of transport, logistics, customs, and regulatory efficiencies that contribute to lower trade cost and improve access to production inputs and consumer goods as well as export markets.

The pandemic-induced supply chain disruptions only underscore the need for a multisector approach to produce a more effective and integrated response to the challenges that surfaced during the peak of the crisis. Congestion and long turnaround times occurred not only at border points but all along transport networks.

As countries begin recovery post-coronavirus disease (COVID-19), more emphasis is being placed on sustainable, resilient, and inclusive growth. Many people are giving priority to adopting environment-friendly practices and people-centered economic policies as countries seek to increase resilience against future pandemics. Trade and transport facilitation measures should be developed with these emerging policy dimensions in mind.

This report provides policy recommendations to achieve an integrated approach to trade and transport facilitation. It reviews regional and multilateral policy documents to identify gaps in provisions and implementation that affect trade costs. It provides recommendations to enhance trade-enabling physical and institutional infrastructure both *at- and beyond-the-border*. The publication also presents a framework and an illustrative case study to help countries assess their trade readiness at national and subnational (trade corridor) levels.

I hope that the report will be helpful to the region's policy makers and trade practitioners who are tasked with reinvigorating trade and making it more inclusive, resilient, and sustainable. Supporting countries to participate in global value chains will benefit people and businesses throughout Asia and the Pacific.

Albert Francis Park
Chief Economist and Director General
Economic Research and Regional Cooperation Department
Asian Development Bank

Acknowledgments

This publication was prepared by the Regional Cooperation and Integration Division (ERCI) of the Economic Research and Regional Cooperation Department (ERCD), Asian Development Bank (ADB), with support from the Regional Cooperation and Integration Thematic Group (RCI-TG) of the Sustainable Development and Climate Change Department, ADB. It was financed by ADB under the Knowledge and Support Technical Assistance for Forward-Looking Trade Facilitation Measures in Asia and the Pacific.

Cyn-Young Park, ERCI Director, provided overall direction and supervision of the report at ADB.

Sanchita Basu-Das, Economist, ERCI, led the study project from conceptualization to research and drafting of the report. Kijin Kim, Senior Economist, ERCI, provided inputs as well as guidance throughout the study period and reviewed the report in all preparation stages. Shubham Gupta, Partner at Deloitte, and Nishant Jain, Associate Director at Deloitte, were part of the study team as ADB consultants to draft the report.

Aileen Pangilinan (RCI-TG), Aleli Rosario (ERCI), Shrenik Shah (Deloitte), and Sravani Tanaya (Deloitte) helped prepare the report in capacities as research assistant, reviewer, and coordinator.

The publication benefited from the valuable insights of Ronald Antonio Butiong, RCI-TG Chief, who also facilitated discussion with regional departments. The study team is thankful to ADB RCI Committee members and Trade Facilitation Subgroup focals for their support and feedback since the project design phase. We acknowledge receiving feedback during the review stage of the draft report and later during a technical presentation session in August 2022 from members of the Southeast Asia Department (Alfredo Perdiguero, Asadullah Sumbal Khan, and Kanya Satyani Sasradipoera; East Asia Department (Zulfia Khamitovna Karimova and Dorothea Lazaro); Central and West Asia Department (Seung Min Lee); Pacific Department (Ashish Narain); and South Asia Department (Thiam Hee Ng and Tadateru Hayashi).

We thank Albert Park, Chief Economist and Director General, ERCD, for his feedback and strong support.

The study team appreciates the opportunity given to present part of the study during the 10th Asia-Pacific Trade Facilitation Forum, co-organized by ADB and ESCAP with Singapore's Ministry of Trade and Industry, held in Singapore in August 2022. The team also organized a hybrid side event on the topic of an integrated approach to trade and transport facilitation—during the

Third Ministerial Conference on Regional Economic Cooperation and Integration in Asia and the Pacific in Bangkok, Thailand, in September 2022—to understand interest and the priorities of the greater community of government, academia, and the private sector. The team appreciates the knowledge received during these events.

The publication was produced with the support of many members within ADB. Sanchita Basu-Das, and Aleli Rosario, Senior Economics Officer in ERCI, conducted the groundwork, and coordinated overall production. Marilyn Aure. Parra helped facilitate discussion among team members and coordinating with different ADB departments throughout the period of study duration. Eric Van Zant edited the manuscript. Josef Ilumin created the cover design. Joe Mark Ganaban did the layout and typesetting. Lawrence Casiraya performed proofreading, with support from Aleli Rosario and Carol Ongchangco. The Printing Services Unit of ADB's Corporate Services Department and the Publishing team of the Department of Communications supported printing and publishing.

Abbreviations

ADB	Asian Development Bank
ASEAN	Association of Southeast Asian Nations
BCP	border-crossing point
CAREC	Central Asia Regional Economic Cooperation Program
CBTA	Cross-Border Transport Agreement
CITA	CAREC Integrated Trade Agenda
GMS	Greater Mekong Subregion
ICT	information and communication technology
LPI	Logistics Performance Index
MSMEs	micro, small, and medium-sized enterprises
NTFC	National Trade Facilitation Committee
OECD	Organisation for Economic Co-operation and Development
OECD TFI	OECD Trade Facilitation Indicators
PRC	People's Republic of China
SASEC	South Asia Subregional Economic Cooperation
SMEs	small and medium-sized enterprises
SPS	sanitary and phytosanitary
TBT	technical barriers to trade
TF	trade facilitation
TFA	Trade Facilitation Agreement
TIR	Transports Internationaux Routiers (International Road Transports)
UNESCAP	United Nations Economic and Social Commission for Asia and the Pacific
WCO	World Customs Organization
WTO	World Trade Organization
WTO TFA	WTO Trade Facilitation Agreement

Executive Summary

Trade has been a key driver of economic growth and poverty reduction. Trade in goods has increased incomes by 24% globally since 1990, and 50% for the poorest 40% of the population.[1] The beneficial links between trade and investment catalyze economic transformation, job creation, and skill development—which supports the 2030 Agenda for Sustainable Development. The unprecedented growth in international trade and interconnectedness of economies has led to globalization of supply chains. Addressing trade barriers has thus become a policy priority of developing countries for several years now. While tariffs have been reduced under multilateral and regional trade regimes, nontariff barriers, in terms of cross-border regulations and related infrastructure, continue to pose challenge. The trade costs associated with nontariff barriers are estimated to be more than double those of tariffs (UNESCAP and UNCTAD 2019).

Reducing trade costs is essential to enable economies to effectively participate in international trade. A recent study by World Trade Organization (WTO) examined bilateral trade costs for 43 countries and 33 sectors between 2000 and 2018 and decomposed the trade costs in five categories: transport and travel costs, information and transaction costs, information and communication technology connectedness, trade policy and regulatory differences, and governance quality (Rubínová and Sebti 2021). The study found that transport and travel costs account the most in the overall trade cost (29% for goods). Trade policy and regulatory differences are the second major component of trade cost in most sectors. Figure 1 shows the breakup of trade costs.   These are even more significant for landlocked countries such as Bhutan, the Lao People's Democratic Republic (Lao PDR), and Mongolia, that rely completely on trading gateways (seaports) outside the country for imports and exports. These countries face challenges from delay in transit, customs inefficiencies, and absence of quality transport infrastructure and related cross-border regulations.

Accordingly, an integrated approach for trade and transport facilitation is essential to improve trade connectivity. This has been discussed in various study reports, such as the World Bank's *Integration of Transport and Trade Facilitation: Selected Regional Case Studies* (2001) and *Lao PDR Trade and Transport Facilitation Assessment* (2014), the Asian Development Bank's (ADB) *Trade And Transport Facilitation Monitoring Mechanism In Bangladesh: Baseline Study* (2017), and the United Nations' Economic Commission for Latin America and the Caribbean's *The Future of Trade and Transport Facilitation: Implications of the WTO Trade Facilitation Agreement* (2014).

---

[1]   See the World Bank website at https://www.worldbank.org/en/topic/trade/overview. Trade refers to trade in merchandise and goods and does not include trade in services unless otherwise mentioned.

Figure 1: Trade Cost Decomposition
(%)

	Trade between low-income economies	Overall trade in goods
Transportation and travel	22	29
Information and transaction	16	16
ICT connectedness	7	4
Trade policy and regulatory differences	24	16
Governance quality	12	9
Others	18	26

ICT = information and communication technology.

Source: World Trade Organization (WTO). 2021. WTO Trade Cost Index: Evolution, Incidence and Determinants. Geneva. https://www.wto.org/english/res_e/reser_e/ersd202106_e.pdf.

The coronavirus disease (COVID-19) pandemic has further highlighted the need for an integrated approach to trade and transport facilitation to enhance trade resilience. The lockdowns and border closures during the height of the pandemic revealed many weaknesses in the trade and transport facilitation ecosystem as it restricted the movement of goods and people. Requirements for testing, driver swap, trailer swap, and transshipment at warehouses introduced to ensure the safety of workers also contributed to bottlenecks for freight. Many countries implemented short-term crisis measures to mitigate the impact, including accelerated deployment of digital tools. Yet, many still lack long-term trade facilitation strategy and plans to enhance preparedness for such future crises.

Trade facilitation guidance needs to be multi dimensional and efficiently implemented. Trade facilitation frameworks need to address elements related to both physical enablers (border infrastructure facilities, transport infrastructure, testing laboratories to comply with standards for trade in goods) and nonphysical enablers (such as cross-border transport procedures, nontariff barriers, bilateral and regional trade and transport agreements, extent of automation/digitization, and crisis management and climate change mitigation measures). Climate change risks and greater inclusivity should be considered inherently within this all-encompassing framework.

Approach and Methodology of the Study

The study adopts a systematic approach of four workstreams. It includes a secondary review of the existing trade facilitation and transport frameworks of different international organizations across geographies (Workstream-1). Gaps within these guidance documents have been identified in the current and future requirements for enhancement of international trade (Workstream-2). Provisions critical to address these gaps have been identified from global best practices and review of the literature. Building on these, a comprehensive group of provisions relevant for holistic and integrated trade and transport facilitation is developed (Workstream-3). Finally, the study's illustrative framework allows assessment of national and subnational readiness through identification of relevant key performance indicators. It presents a case study on a section of the Southern Economic Corridor across Thailand and Cambodia for ease of understanding (Workstream-4).

Figure 2: Flowchart on the Workstream Approach

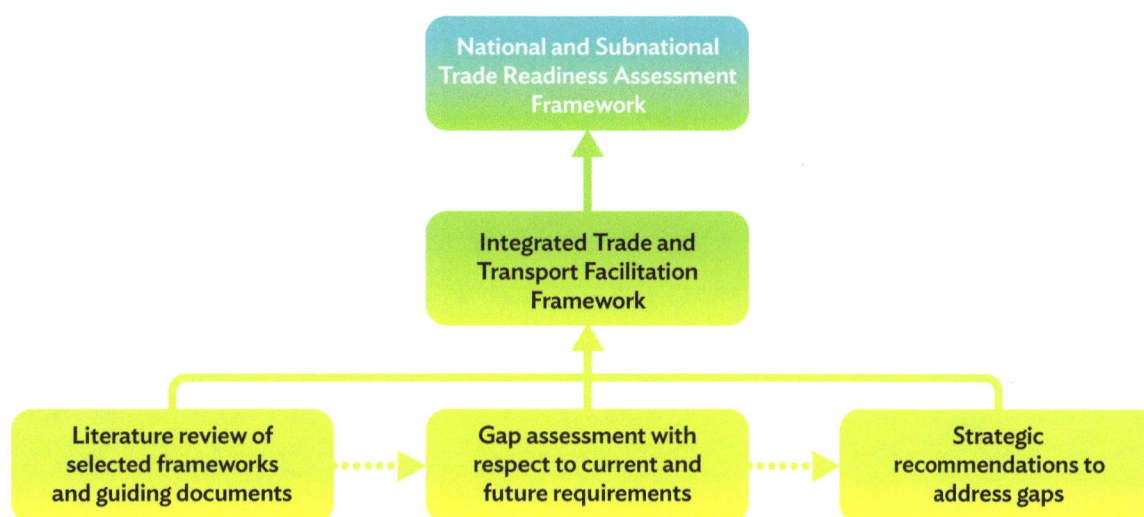

Source: Study team's illustration.

Workstream-1: Literature Review of Selected Frameworks and Guiding Documents

Trade and transport facilitation elements are clubbed across six clusters of themes. The study reviewed and evaluated eight international- and regional-level trade and transport facilitation strategic frameworks and documents, briefly discussed in section 2.1. Based on the review, it identified six clusters of 11 themes containing 97 enabling provisions relevant for the subject. Transport agreements and conventions are reviewed and discussed separately to complement and strengthen the analysis.

The extent of coverage and emphasis on respective clusters and themes varied significantly across guiding frameworks and documents. This is illustrated in Table 1. For a particular theme, the trade and transport facilitation document with highest relative coverage has been indicated through a 100%-solid Harvey ball, and progressive reduction in coverage is depicted through corresponding hollowness of the Harvey ball. For example, the World Trade Organization Trade Facilitation Agreement (WTO TFA) covers the Simplification and Harmonization theme in relatively

Table 1: Topic Coverage across Trade and Transport Facilitation Frameworks

Relative Coverage of Thematic Clusters across TTF Frameworks		WTO TFA	SASEC OP 2016–2025	CAREC CITA 2030	ASEAN TTF	ADB-ESCAP Study	UN TF Survey	WB TTFA	GMS TTF–AP
Customs Procedures and Formalities	Simplification and Harmonization	●	◐	◐	◕	◕	◕	◐	◕
	Digitization	◐	◕	◔	◐	◕	●	◐	◔
SPS/TBT	Standardization	◐	●	◐	◐	◐	●	○	◔
Stakeholder Coordination	Institutional Coordination/Capacity Building	●	◕	◐	○	◐	◕	◐	◔
	Stakeholder Involvement	◕	○	◐	●	◐	○	◕	○
Transit and Cross-Border Facilities	Transit	◐	◔	◕	◕	◐	●	○	◕
	Cross-border facilities	○	●	◐	○	○	○	◕	○
Transport	Transport Infrastructure	○	◐	○	○	○	○	●	○
	Trade Finance	○	○	◔	◔	●	●	◔	○
Sustainability and Resilience	SME Trade Facilitation	○	○	◔	○	◔	●	○	○
	Sustainable Trade	○	○	○	○	○	●	○	○

● — Maximum coverage to least coverage → ○, * = Survey, High coverage , Medium coverage , Low coverage .

ADB CAREC = Asian Development Bank Central Asia Regional Economic Cooperation, ASEAN = Association of Southeast Asian Nations, GMS = Greater Mekong Subregion, RC = regional cooperation, SASEC = South Asia Subregional Economic Cooperation, SME = small and medium-sized enterprises, SPS/TBT = sanitary and phytosanitary/technical barriers to trade, TF = trade facilitation, UNESCAP = United Nations Economic and Social Commission for Asia and the Pacific, WTO TFA = World Trade Organization Trade Facilitation Agreement.

Source: Data from various guiding frameworks and documents including the WTO TFA, ADB SASEC Operational Plan, ADB CAREC Integrated Trade Agenda, Greater Mekong Subregion Trade and Transport Facilitation, World Bank Trade and Transport Facilitation Assessment, United Nations Digital and Sustainable Trade Facilitation: Global Report 2021, and study team's estimates.

maximum depth. As such, it has been indicated with a 100%-solid Harvey ball and other frameworks and guidance documents with relatively hollower Harvey balls denoting lesser coverage.

Workstream-2: Gap Assessment of Current and Future Requirements

Mapping the identified clusters and themes to the WTO trade cost composition, it is found that clusters and themes impacting the bulk of the trade cost are covered in relatively less width and depth across existing trade and transport facilitation frameworks and guidance documents. These themes include Stakeholder Involvement, Cross-Border Facilities, Transport, Trade Finance, small and medium-sized enterprise (SME) Trade Facilitation, and Sustainable Trade Facilitation.

Table 2 shows the summary of the gap analysis of coverage of provisions related to trade and transport facilitation themes across literature reviewed in this study.

Workstream-3: Strategic Recommendations to Address Gaps

Provisions present across the reviewed literature were combined to summarize them into a comprehensive trade and transport facilitation guidance table. **While gaps in the availability of provisions were observed for themes such as Sustainable Trade and Transport Infrastructure, provisions for other themes were identified largely to have implementation efficacy issues.** The following recommendations are thus provided for governments and other key stakeholder considerations:

Adding multidimensionality: New provisions for the Sustainability and Resilience cluster need to be included. The Sustainable Trade theme under this cluster could include disaster and crisis management, climate change mitigation, and gender sensitivity, which form a large group of important factors that impact the trade cost. Key provisions added include (i) development of a three-phase crisis response and resilience framework for covering immediate response, recovery mechanisms, and building resilience; (ii) incentivizing new and efficient transport technologies, e.g., using sustainable and alternative fuels and substitution for more carbon-efficient alternative means of transportation; (iii) strengthening existing institutions, i.e., the National Trade Facilitation Committee (NTFC) for comprehensive discussion of trade and transport facilitation measures; and (iv) developing a built-in mechanism to mitigate climate change risks and greater inclusivity through an equity in trade environment for women and SME traders.[2]

---

[2]   NTFCs were created as part of the WTO TFA to coordinate trade facilitation reforms at the national level. Each committee's institutional arrangements and responsibilities can be found in Article 23 of the TFA. Sections 3.2.3 and 3.2.4 detail the role of the institution.

Table 2: Mapping Determinants of Trade Cost with Overall Coverage of Trade and Transport Facilitation Themes across Existing Guidance Documents

Trade Cost Composition for Goods (WTO) / Key TTF Thematic Clusters	Customs Procedures and Formalities		SPS/TBT	Stakeholder Coordination		Transit and Cross-Border Facilities		Transport	Trade Finance	Sustainability and Resilience	
	Simplification and Harmonization	Digitization	Standardization	Institutional Coordination/ Capacity Building	Stakeholder Involvement	Transit	Cross-Border Facilities	Transport Infrastructure	Trade Finance	SME Trade Facilitation	Sustainable Trade
Transportation and Travel — 29%					Medium	High	Medium	Low	Medium	Low	Low
Information and Transaction — 16%	High	High			Medium			Low			Low
ICT Connectedness — 4%	High	High		High							
Trade Policy and Regulatory Differences — 16%	High	High	High	High		High					Low
Governance Quality — 9%				High	Medium						
Others — 26%									Medium	Low	Low

Legend: High coverage (green), Medium coverage (yellow), Low coverage (orange).

ICT = information and communication technology, SME = small and medium-sized enterprise, SPS/TBT = sanitary and phytosanitary/technical barriers to trade, TTF = transport and trade facilitation, WTO = World Trade Organization.

Source: WTO Trade Cost Index and Its Determinants and study team's estimates.

Figure 3: Recommendations for Integrated Trade and Transport Facilitation

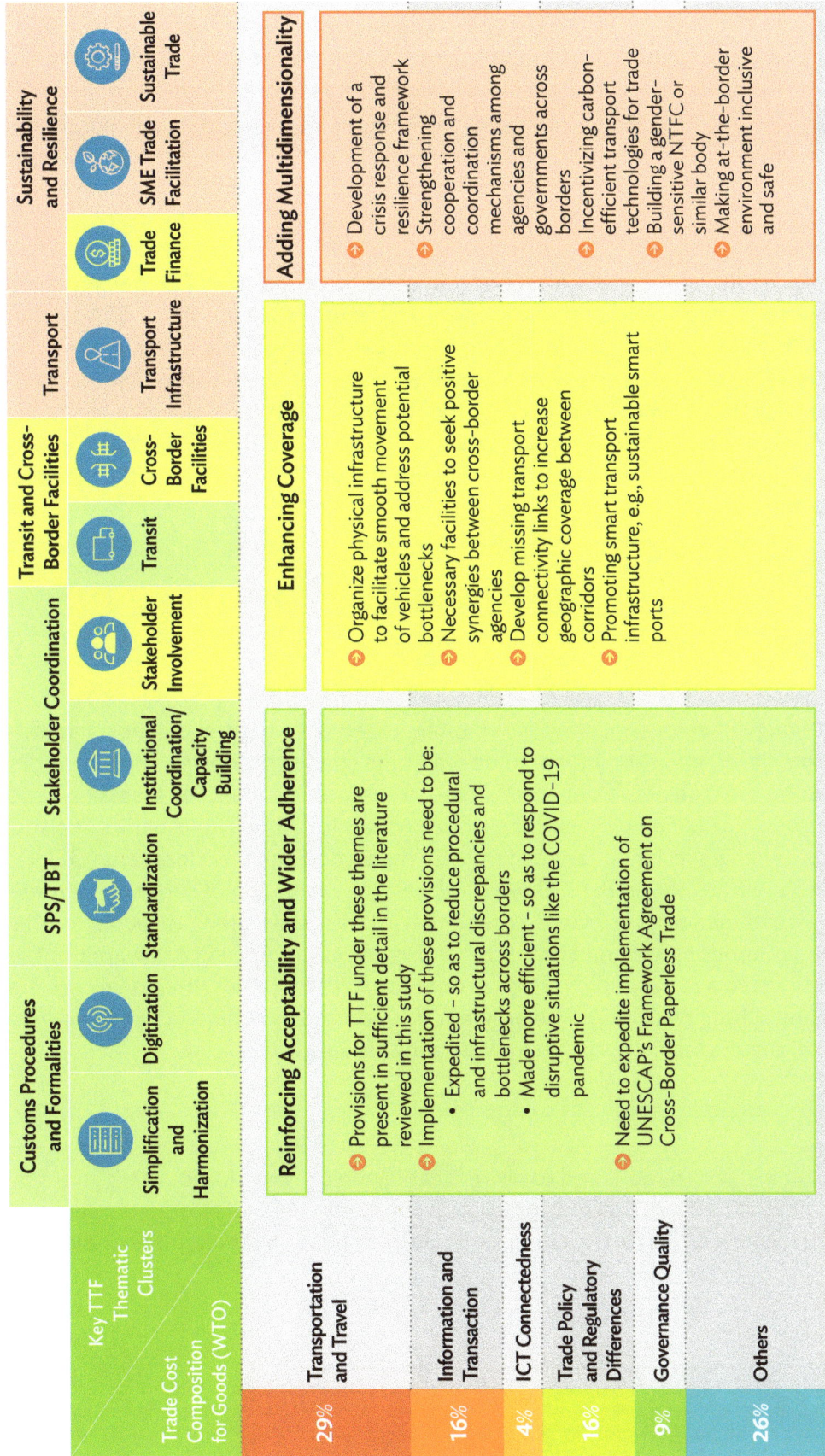

Trade Cost Composition for Goods (WTO)	Key TTF Thematic Clusters	Customs Procedures and Formalities		SPS/TBT	Stakeholder Coordination		Transit and Cross-Border Facilities		Transport	Sustainability and Resilience		
		Simplification and Harmonization	Digitization	Standardization	Institutional Coordination/Capacity Building	Stakeholder Involvement	Transit	Cross-Border Facilities	Transport Infrastructure	Trade Finance	SME Trade Facilitation	Sustainable Trade
29%	Transportation and Travel											
16%	Information and Transaction											
4%	ICT Connectedness											
16%	Trade Policy and Regulatory Differences											
9%	Governance Quality											
26%	Others											

Reinforcing Acceptability and Wider Adherence

- ↻ Provisions for TTF under these themes are present in sufficient detail in the literature reviewed in this study
- ↻ Implementation of these provisions need to be:
  - • Expedited – so as to reduce procedural and infrastructural discrepancies and bottlenecks across borders
  - • Made more efficient – so as to respond to disruptive situations like the COVID-19 pandemic
- ↻ Need to expedite implementation of UNESCAP's Framework Agreement on Cross-Border Paperless Trade

Enhancing Coverage

- ↻ Organize physical infrastructure to facilitate smooth movement of vehicles and address potential bottlenecks
- ↻ Necessary facilities to seek positive synergies between cross-border agencies
- ↻ Develop missing transport connectivity links to increase geographic coverage between corridors
- ↻ Promoting smart transport infrastructure, e.g., sustainable smart ports

Adding Multidimensionality

- ↻ Development of a crisis response and resilience framework
- ↻ Strengthening cooperation and coordination mechanisms among agencies and governments across borders
- ↻ Incentivizing carbon-efficient transport technologies for trade
- ↻ Building a gender-sensitive NTFC or similar body
- ↻ Making at-the-border environment inclusive and safe

High coverage , Medium coverage , Low coverage .

COVID-19 = coronavirus disease, ICT = information and communication technology, NTFC = National Trade Facilitation Committee, SME= small and medium-sized enterprise, SPS/TBT = sanitary and phytosanitary/technical barriers to trade, TTF = transport and trade facilitation, UNESCAP = United Nations Economic and Social Commission for Asia and the Pacific, WTO = World Trade Organization.

Source: World Trade Organization Trade Cost Index and Its Determinants and study team's estimates.

Enhancing coverage: Provisions for clusters on transport and transit and cross-border facilities need strengthening of coverage of the issues under them. The study identifies key aspects important to ensuring the effectiveness of implementation of the provisions in these clusters. They include, among others, modernization of border infrastructure, collaboration among cross-border agencies, focus on compatibility, uniformity of standards and last-mile coverage in the development of transport infrastructure, development of intermodal hubs, and development of smart transport systems.

Reinforcing acceptability and wider adherence: Implementation of WTO measures and other agreements need to be expedited and made more efficient. While the WTO TFA provides detailed guidance for some of the procedural "at-the-border" issues of trade facilitation, evidence reviewed in the study suggests that even when armed with such detailed knowledge and guidance, countries had to undertake ad hoc measures to respond to trade disruptions which emerge in crises like the COVID-19 pandemic. A key lesson derived from these experiences is to focus on expedited and efficient implementation of provisions of framework agreements for enhancing preparedness for specific disruptions.

Workstream-4: National and Subnational Trade Readiness Assessment Framework

This workstream brings all outputs of previous chapters together to suggest diagnostic frameworks for national (country level) and subnational trade readiness (trade corridors). The indicators are identified to measure the readiness using the framework discussed earlier. For assessing national readiness, indicators are obtained from existing global indices from the World Bank's Logistics Performance Index, the Organisation for Economic Co-operation and Development (OECD) Trade Facilitation Indicators, World Bank Open Data, etc. For evaluation of subnational trade corridors, use of a combination of primary and secondary data is suggested.[3] A section of the Southern Economic Corridor spanning Thailand and Cambodia, comprising Aranyaprathet and Poipet, has been selected as a case study. This corridor forms part of the subregional cooperation of the Greater Mekong Subregion (GMS). The program is supported by ADB and hence information at trade corridor level is more readily available from existing studies.

National trade readiness assessment framework

To obtain a measurable, comparable, and easily replicable perspective of a country's strength across trade and transport facilitation clusters (as detailed in the study), 46 indicators from seven global indices have been identified.[4] To create a uniform scale of evaluation for identified indicators,

---

[3] A sample questionnaire is provided in Appendix 5 to guide the document for the same.
[4] These 46 indicators have been obtained from the seven global indices such as World Bank's Logistics Performance Index, the OECD Trade Facilitation Indicators, and so on, for measuring national trade readiness. The indices are a group of indicators based on relevant themes; e.g., logistics performance is the theme measured by World Bank's Logistics Performance Index, which is eventually measured by multiple indicators such as efficiency of customs and border management clearance ("customs"), quality of logistics services, etc.

the framework recommends calculating percentiles for a country in focus for the global, regional, and subregional samples.[5]

This study, in comparing the Thailand and Cambodia cases, presents a comparative scale for "state of readiness" across all six clusters. Figure 4 illustrates the first cluster of the study—Customs Procedures and Formalities. Thailand is positioned above the 50th percentile in majority of the indicators in all three samples, e.g., in OECD indicator G8: Single Window Implementation, Thailand scores above the 50th percentile in global, Asian, and Southeast Asian samples. For Cambodia, the performance of the majority of the indicators for the cluster is below the 50th percentile for the global, Asian, and Southeast Asian samples. For example, for the same OECD indicator on single window implementation, Cambodia scores below the 50th percentile in all the three samples.

Figure 4: National Trade Readiness Assessment: Customs Procedures and Formalities Cluster

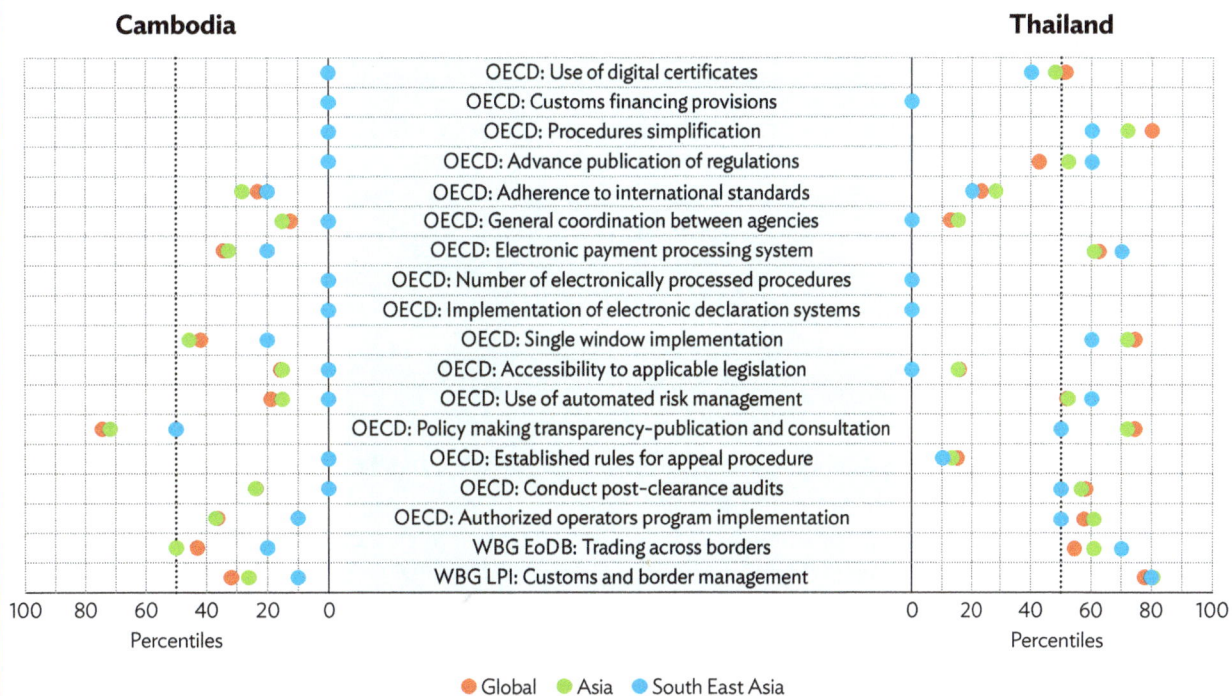

OECD = Organization for Economic Co-operation and Development, WBG EoDB = World Bank Group Ease of Doing Business, WBG LPI = World bank Group Logistics Performance Indicator.
Sources: Reports published on respective indices: details provided in Appendix 3; study team's estimates.

---

[5] For a country like Thailand, the regional sample is Asia and subregional sample is Southeast Asia.

Subnational trade readiness assessment framework

Subnational readiness aims to assess a trade gateway across countries (border-crossing point at land, port, airport, etc.) in its process efficiency, major delays, quality of services (lead time and cost) and at-the-border/cross-border infrastructure.[6] Forty-three key indicators across the six key clusters (detailed in the previous section) have been identified for developing the subnational trade readiness assessment framework. Data for the indicators can be obtained through secondary sources such as publications, media reports, research papers, etc. Where values for some of the indicators are not available from secondary sources, information can be obtained through primary consultations (a sample questionnaire is provided in Appendix 5 to serve as a guidance document for the same).

This report, as an illustration, looked at the Southern Economic Corridor across Thailand and Cambodia, including the border ports of Aranyaprathet and Poipet. As this corridor forms part of the subregional cooperation of the Greater Mekong Subregion (GMS), supported by ADB, information on many indicators is available from existing studies, such as the World Bank's *Cambodia Trade Corridor Performance Assessment* and ADB's *Breaking Barriers: Leveraging Mongolia's Transport and Logistics Sector*, etc. (World Bank 2014, ADB 2018).

For the clusters Customs Procedures and Formalities, and Stakeholder Coordination, the study has identified 12 indicators to measure subnational readiness. The illustrative analysis of the Aranyaprathet border-crossing point (BCP) in Thailand and Poipet BCP in Cambodia showcases that Aranyaprathet BCP performs better across indicators than Poipet BCP. This is indicated by five green cells (above comparator performance) out of 12 indicators for Aranyaprathet, whereas Poipet has only two green cells out of 12 indicators. Similarly, for the Transit and Cross-Border Facilities, and SPS TBT clusters, Poipet performs better across indicators, which is indicated by 10 green cells out of 12 indicators; whereas Aranyaprathet has 6 indicators across which it is above comparator and for the clusters Transport Infrastructure and Sustainability and Resilience, Aranyaprathet has 3 areas of above average performance out of 19 indicators, whereas Poipet is marked by only 1 green cell.

Table 3 illustrates the assessment for Customs Procedures and Formalities and Stakeholder Coordination.

Illustrative policy recommendations from the case studies

Based on the findings of the Thailand and Cambodia and gap identification, Tables 4 and 5 detail illustrative recommendations to improve trade facilitation through the gateway. The study has identified those for enhancing trade and transport facilitation in the two countries. The issues have been consolidated into areas where either the country or BCP falls below average or is below the 50th percentile. Even when the indicators for either country are already above comparator or more than the 50th percentile have not been specifically evaluated, these cases will have scope for improvement.

---

6   A BCP, can be a land border, airports, etc., having basic customs infrastructure or may have a fully integrated facility border.

Table 3: Illustrative Subnational Readiness Assessment for Custom Procedures and Formalities and Stakeholders Coordination

Parameters	Information Requirement for Evaluation	Aranyaprathet	Poipet	Comparators
Customs Procedures and Formalities and Stakeholder Coordination				
Customs Clearance Process	Average time taken for import clearance			Average import clearance time is 2 hours 12 minutes in Thailand (Aranyaprathet)
	Percent of import declarations cleared electronically			Presence of 100% electronic clearance of import documents
	Average time taken for export clearance			Average export clearance time is 3 hours 52 minutes in the Lao PDR
	Percent of export declarations cleared electronically			Presence of 100% electronic clearance of export documents
	Rate of duplication of bureaucratic activities			Presence of electronic data exchange system and single-window mechanism to eliminate duplication
	Border-clearance cost			Average border-import-clearance cost for ASEAN as per trading across border Indicators—$105.3
	Provision of digital payments			Presence of operational e-payment system of tariffs and duties
Pre-shipment Inspection	Time taken for pre-shipment physical inspection			Time for physical inspection should not exceed 1 day (country average as per WBG LPI)
	Percentage of physical Inspection			Physical inspection should not exceed more than 5% (probability by WBG trading across borders)
Solicitation of Informal Payments	Prevalence of informal payments for cargo clearance/checkpoints/weighbridge stations/traffic stops, etc.			Transparent and digital procedures to ensure 0% informal payments
Cross-Border Coordination	Synchronization of border timings, clearance procedures			Border-time harmonization requirement for seamless cargo transit across borders
	Presence of international agreements and memorandum of understanding			Presence of CBTA/MOUs/agreements to allow ease of clearance process and allow 100% of vehicles for cross-border transportation

Above comparator , Below comparator .

ASEAN = Association of Southeast Asian Nations, CBTA = Cross-Border Transport Agreement, Lao PDR = Lao People's Democratic Republic, MOU = memorandum of understanding, WBG LPI = World Bank Group Logistics Performance Index.

Sources: World Bank's Logistics Performance Index. https://lpi.worldbank.org/; World Bank Group. 2014. Cambodia Trade Corridor Performance Assessment. https://openknowledge.worldbank.org/handle/10986/20763, Asian Development Bank. 2018. Leveraging Mongolia's Transport and Logistics Sector. Manila and study team's estimates.

Table 4: National-Level Illustrative Policy Recommendations for Cambodia and Thailand

Sl. No.	Identified Issue	Illustrative Recommendations	
		Cambodia	Thailand
Key Recommendations on Customs Procedures and Formalities			
1	Low filing of digital certificates due to lack of proper implementation of electronic declaration system and electronic processed procedures	● Fiscal and nonfiscal incentives to encourage digital filing of certificates by the traders to reduce dwelling time for cargo at the trading gateways ● Operationalization and implementation of advanced electronic declaration system to promote paperless transactions and electronic procedures	
2	Lack of adequate financing provision	● Provision for funding schemes, particularly for small and medium-sized enterprises (SMEs) and women traders ● Conduct workshops and awareness-training sessions to disseminate information on the custom financing provision	
3	Low adherence to international standards	● National-level policy provisions in line with international trade process standards to improve level of compliance	
4	Lack of proper provisions for advance publication of regulations	● Provisions for mandatory notification system on any changes in trade regulations and process by the National Bank of Cambodia, Ministry of Commerce	* (Please see end note of the table for this reference)
5	Limited implementation of Automated Risk Management System (consignments identified as Red Lane by ASYCUDA are manually entered into the system by frontline customs officials so that Risk Management Unit (RMU) officials can assess the detailed risks further)	● Upgrade Customs Risk Management Database System (CRMDS 2011) to ensure objectivity in facilitation and enforcement, and expedite release of low-risk cargo ● Implementation of CRMDS in all of the border checkpoints in Cambodia (currently implemented in 10 main checkpoints)	*
6	Electronic payment processing system	● Mechanism to implement digital payment interface (e-payment module) for trade related payments in Cambodia	*
7	Lack of single-window implementation	● Implement and upgrade the Cambodia National Single Window System, integrated with all concerned regulatory agencies providing clearances/approvals to the traders	*
8	Lack of proper rules on appeal procedures and lack of accessibility to applicable legislation	● Introduce initiative for a simplified appeal procedure with provisions of time periods of the procedures. ● Provide information on available legislation to SMEs and women traders through advance publications/SMS services, etc.	
9	Outdated manual for post-clearance audits	● Development of up-to-date dedicated manual for post clearance audit to create an environment of increased compliance and enhance facilitation of importers and exporters (current manual is of the year 2008)	*

continued on next page

Table 4 *continued*

Sl. No.	Identified Issue	Illustrative Recommendations	
		Cambodia	Thailand
10	Limited implementation for authorized economic operators	➔ Upgrade the existing Best Trader Incentive Mechanism for complete implementation as per 2023 strategy for customs reforms and modernization ➔ Introduce policy provisions for trade and regulation to facilitate special MSME Authorized Economic Operators accreditation (that require less stringent criteria) for the benefit of compliant trade	*
Key Recommendations on SPS TBT			
11	Absence of required mutual recognition agreements (SPS standards for certain agricultural products are applied arbitrarily and without prior notification in Thailand)	➔ Initiate dialogues for mutual recognition agreements with major trading partners to recognize each other's competent conformity assessment bodies thereby reducing nontariff barriers ➔ Development of appropriate country-level legislation for the signing of mutual recognition agreements	
Key Recommendations on Transit and Cross-Border Facilities			
12	Low rates of pre-arrival processing	➔ Encourage traders through workshops to undertake pre-shipment testing for all consignments to avoid lag at border-crossing and for advance filling of documents to reduce dwell time of cargo at the BCP ➔ Include a provision in the country-level Customs Act to allow customs clearance of containerized export cargo at factory premises/off-border clearances prior to its movement to the respective BCPs	
		➔ Simplification of the existing advance ruling procedures in Cambodia	➔ Increase the rate of pre-arrival processing at land ports in Thailand through advanced electronic manifests and advance payment of duties and taxes by sensitization of importers and exporters on the processes
Key Recommendations on Stakeholder Consultation			
13	Limited consultations between stakeholders and internal coordination of domestic border agencies, and lack of effective control delegation and institutionalized mechanism to improve interagency coordination	➔ Policy upgrade for strengthening and institutionalizing the National Trade Facilitation Committee (NTFC) to represent an exhaustive range of internal stakeholders that have a role in trade and transport (including SMEs, women and private sector) ➔ Conduct annual policy dialogues to improve collaboration between at the at-the-border and behind-the-border agencies and the private sector ➔ Set short-term and long-term goals for NTFCs to achieve 100% interagency coordination within a time frame	
14	Lack of cross-border harmonization, coordination, and infrastructure use	➔ Increase cross-border coordination through establishment of memorandum of understanding, initiatives on joint infrastructure projects, and cross-border agreements by initiating discussion with concerned authorities of the member countries ➔ Mutually share and accept weighment slips, accompanied by weighment of select import cargo (subject to risk parameters) ➔ Development of regional single window system to enable exchange of key documents between Cambodia and Thailand to further expedite cargo clearance process and reduce paperwork	

continued on next page

Table 4 *continued*

Sl. No.	Identified Issue	Illustrative Recommendations	
		Cambodia	Thailand
15	Automated processing of customs declaration not operational 24/7	Initiate discussions with concerned authorities in Cambodia and Thailand to ensure adherence to 24/7 operations at all BCPs	
16	Lack of provisions for cross-border staff training program	Develop and implement policy mandates for joint staff training programs of Thailand and Cambodia to enhance collaboration and information exchange of cross-border processes between the countries	
Key Recommendations on Transport Infrastructure			
17	Absence of tracking and tracing of consignments	To ensure better monitoring of the movement of import/export cargo vehicles along the transit route and take immediate measures, in the event of any deviation/tampering of such vehicles, it is suggested to explore installation of e-seal on the Cambodia registered vehicles subject to evaluation of its commercial viability Explore deployment of a tracking system to facilitate cargo reconciliation	*
18	Lack of quality trade and transport infrastructure at the border	Develop detailed report to undertake construction related activities to augment existing facilities and to create new facilities for trade and transport, e.g., augmentation of internal roads, parking chassis, cold storage facilities, etc.	*
Key Recommendations on Sustainability and Resilience			
19	Lack of efficient trade facilitation measures for women	Implement gender-responsive trade facilitation policy measures and digital tools (promoting contactless trade) to eliminate gender-based barriers (time constraints, costs of burdensome procedures, discrimination and harassment) at borders Build gender-sensitive NTFCs through training sessions Provision for conducting information sessions (through NTFC/other committees/bodies) for informal women traders to provide fact-based insights and to promote women entrepreneurs in the trade and transport sector Adopt a client service charter with a code of conduct for public agents, stating the responsibilities and obligations of administrations toward women traders. Such charters should embody awareness and protection of women's rights, contributing to achieving the Sustainable Development Goals and the declaration on gender equality and diversity in customs of the World Customs Organization, as well as principles of good governance and integrity in customs Provision for favorable tax regime and trade facilitation schemes for women and informal traders Construction activities for appropriate gender-sensitive at-the-border facilities (sanitation facilities such as restroom, bathroom, accommodation, etc.) Establishment of complaint mechanism (grievance redressal mechanism) for victims of gender-based discrimination at borders.	

continued on next page

Table 4 *continued*

Sl. No.	Identified Issue	Illustrative Recommendations	
		Cambodia	**Thailand**
20	Lack of efficient trade environment for SMEs	● Provision for deferred tax/subsidized tax and duties for SMEs for expedited shipments ● Application of targeted compliance management approach (under risk management system), for operators that are SMEs, that favors efforts to assist them to comply rather than to penalize them for noncompliance ● Trade procedures information dissemination to SMEs through regular online publication/mobile service, etc. ● Provision for technical consultation and training services to SMEs on registering and using the single window facility	

ASYCUDA = Automated System for Customs Data, BCP = border-crossing point, CBTA = Cross-Border Transport Agreement, MOU = memorandum of understanding, MSME = micro, small, and medium-sized enterprise, SMEs = small and medium-sized enterprises, SMS = short messaging service.

Note: Recommendations have not been provided for areas where Thailand scores more than the 50th percentile; however, scope may remain for strengthening these indicators for the country.

Sources: United Nations Economic and Social Commission for Asia and the Pacific (UNESCAP). 2016. Making the WTO Trade Facilitation Agreement Work for SMEs. https://www.unescap.org/sites/default/files/MakingWTOTFAWorkforSMEs.pdf; United Nations Conference on Trade and Development (UNCTAD). 2022. Policy Brief No. 98. https://unctad.org/system/files/official-document/presspb2022d6_en.pdf; Asian Development Bank (ADB). 2021. *Strengthening Trade Along the Dhaka–Kolkata Route*. Manila. https://www.adb.org/sites/default/files/publication/755651/strengthening-trade-dhaka-kolkata-route.pdf.

Table 5: Subnational Policy Recommendations for Aranyaprathet and Poipet

Sl. No.	Identified Issue	Illustrative Recommendations	
		Aranyaprathet (Thailand)	**Poipet** (Cambodia)
Key Recommendations on Soft Infrastructure			
1	Existence of practice of manual submission of supporting documents for securing approvals which increases the cargo clearance time and trade costs	● Online submission of all documents should be encouraged to facilitate advance filing of declarations through conducting workshops for sensitization/awareness creation among the traders as well as the customs officials to encourage the practice of online submission of all documents	
2	Prevalence of process duplication at the borders	*	● Operationalize national single window system integrated with all concerned regulatory agencies providing clearances/approvals to the traders ● Integrate various existing systems (on either side of the border) on a common digital platform along with development of requisite regulatory framework to enable trade, transport, and commercial data to be exchanged electronically among various government agencies and other key stakeholders
3	Lack of appropriate digital tool for customs-related payments	*	● Design, develop, and implement digital payment interface for trade-related payments at Poipet

continued on next page

Table 5 *continued*

SI. No.	Identified Issue	Illustrative Recommendations	
		Aranyaprathet (Thailand)	Poipet (Cambodia)
4	Presence of high rates of physical Inspection	Implementation of advanced information-technology-driven risk management system to reduce physical inspection rate and time both at Aranyaprathet and Poipet	
5	Limited truck-exchange capacity at the borders	Amend the existing bilateral MOU under the CBTA to allow 100% of vehicles to cross-border Implement Motor Vehicles Agreement across Thailand and Cambodia	
6	Use of traditional fuel trucks	Public policies to adopt use of sustainable e-vehicles for the purpose of trade to reduce trade-related carbon footprint Sensitization of trucking companies through workshops/sessions on the benefits of adopting environment-friendly practices Joint regulatory intervention between Cambodia and Thailand to mandate a percentage of electric vehicles for trade	
Key Recommendations on Hard Infrastructure			
7	High traffic congestion at the BCP	Augmentation of the identified road stretches in number of lanes/construction of roads on a greenfield basis on both sides Construction of an additional gate within the premises to facilitate (i) movement of all cargo vehicles within the customs premises and (ii) passenger movement only at the existing zero point	
8	Lack of warehousing and transloading facilities, parking area, etc.	Conduct feasibility studies and prepare detailed report to undertake construction activities for the development of intermodal transshipment facilities Initiate discussions with the concerned agencies to expedite development of requisite infrastructure such as warehouse, and augment parking area to accommodate 2,000 vehicles Implementation of an online parking management system providing real-time information on availability of parking slots at the BCPs to reduce waiting time and associated costs Develop detailed report for augmenting internal roads and set up adequate halting, as well as maintenance/repair facilities enroute to the BCP on both sides, banking facility, electronic weighbridges, inspection sheds, etc., through feasibility assessment	
9	Presence of compulsory transloading at the borders	Upgrade the CBTA bilateral MOU to allow 100% of the vehicles for cross-border transport without transloading[a] Simplification of process to obtain license to drive through member country Sensitization of the trucking companies through workshops on the process of obtaining the license	
10	Absence of custom bonded warehouses	Initiate discussion with customs officials and conduct feasibility study to develop custom bonded warehouses at Aranyaprathet and Poipet for improving trade Development of a dedicated "export hub" in Aranyaprathet BCP and Poipet BCP which will allow direct entry of export cargo trucks	
11	Lack of operational rail line for trade of goods	Develop detailed report for construction of railway infrastructure such as track, railway sidings, goods yards, import inspection zone, etc., to facilitate import of cargo traffic from Bangkok to Phnom Penh through Aranyaprathet and Poipet and vice versa to reduce trade and logistics cost	

continued on next page

Table 5 *continued*

Sl. No.	Identified Issue	Illustrative Recommendations	
		Aranyaprathet (Thailand)	Poipet (Cambodia)
12	Lack of initiatives on sustainability and inclusiveness	In line with recommendations on national readiness (Table 4 of the Executive Summary), implementing agencies at Aranyaprathet and Poipet need to align their action plans in line with the national-level policies around SME inclusiveness, gender equity, and sustainability of trade facilitation measures	

BCP = border-crossing point, CBTA = Cross-Border Transport Agreement, EV = electric vehicle, MOU = memorandum of understanding, SME = small and medium-sized enterprise.

a The CBTA is a single comprehensive legal instrument that includes all of the nonphysical measures for cross-border land transport. Under the CBTA, vehicles, drivers, goods, and passengers will be allowed to cross national borders through the Greater Mekong Subregion (GMS) road transport system. The agreement promotes the elimination of intermediary stops or transshipment, as well as promoting the reduction in the amount of time spent in crossing borders. Increasing the number of border checkpoints that are implementing the CBTA will help maximize the effectiveness of the GMS transport networks. The CBTA complements the existing physical infrastructure of the GMS countries.

Note: Recommendations have not been provided for the areas of above comparator performance; however, scope may remain for strengthening these indicators for the BCP.

Source: Asian Development Bank. 2021. *Strengthening Trade Along the Dhaka–Kolkata Route*. Manila. https://www.adb.org/sites/default/files/publication/755651/strengthening-trade-dhaka-kolkata-route.pdf.

1. Introduction

With increasing globalization and proliferation of global and regional value chains, international merchandise trade has grown significantly.[1] Developing economies are connected to international supply chains in imports and exports. To cater to rising cross-border trade, governments need to ensure efficient, fast, and reliable border-crossing and clearance procedures, known as trade facilitation.

Trade facilitation does not have a single definition, but in general constitutes a set of policies to reduce the cost of imports and exports. The World Trade Organization (WTO) defines it as "simplification and harmonization of international trade procedures," addressing logistics issues of moving goods across borders (WTO n.d.). The United Nations Centre for Trade Facilitation and Electronic Business (UN/CEFACT) provides a broader definition and mentions it as "the simplification, standardization, and harmonization of procedures and associated information flows required to move goods from seller to buyer and to make payment" (UNECE n.d.). A much broader definition covers the larger ecosystem in which international trade happens, including transparency of regulatory rules and harmonization of and conformation to international or regional standards.

Understanding of trade facilitation can be expanded further to cover transport infrastructure and facilitation as it is the customs efficiency, regulations, and improved transport connectivity that enhances international trade. Currently, while trade facilitation in regional and multilateral documents often covers measures related to simplification and modernization of customs processes to facilitate time-bound export-import processes, the discussion of transport facilitation is covered separately in transport agreements and conventions. Building transport infrastructure is often a part of national development plans. To overcome the issue of fragmented discussion of trade-enabling infrastructure and regulations, trade facilitation should cover all-encompassing measures ranging from physical infrastructure (border infrastructure facilities, transport infrastructure, information technology, testing laboratories to comply with standards for trade in goods) and nonphysical measures (cross-border transport procedures, nontariff barriers, bilateral and regional trade and transport agreements, extent of automation/digitization, and climate change mitigation measures).

---

[1]   See UNCTADSTAT: Merchandise: Total trade and share, annual https://unctadstat.unctad.org/wds/ReportFolders/reportFolders.aspx (accessed September 2022).

Transport costs form a large share of overall cost of trade.

In the last 2 decades, countries around the world have seen significant growth in international trade and rise in development of global or regional value chains, implying that goods are not produced in one but multiple countries. Around 70% of global trade involves such supply chains, where raw materials and intermediate goods move along international borders multiple times before being converted to the final product for the end user (OECD n.d.). For example, manufacturing a mobile phone involves over 200 suppliers spread across 43 countries (Ross 2020).

Reducing trade costs becomes essential for enabling economies to effectively participate in regional and global value chains. While average applied tariffs have declined or eliminated since the establishment of the WTO, attention has increasingly shifted to nontariff measures (Kurmanalieva 2020). The trade cost associated with nontariff measures is estimated to be more than double those of tariffs (UNESCAP and UNCTAD 2019). Besides, transport cost is included as a key determinant of international trade (Vidya and Taghizadeh-Hesary 2020). Bilateral trade costs are strongly influenced by factors such as logistics and connectivity (Arvis et al. 2015).

According to the WTO Global Trade Cost Index and Its Determinants, although global trade costs declined 15% during 2008–2018,[2] (WTO Trade Cost Index n.d.), transport and travel costs continue to be a substantial proportion of total trade cost for both goods and services. Trade policy and regulatory differences are the second major component of trade costs, accounting for 16%–18%. For trade between low-income economies, trade policy and regulatory differences and transportation and travel costs account for 24% and 22%, respectively, of total trade cost. The study decomposes the WTO Global Trade Cost Index into five policy-relevant components: transport and travel costs, information and transaction costs, information and communication technology (ICT) connectedness, trade policy and regulatory differences, and governance quality.

The trade cost decomposition across the determinants is detailed in Figure 5 and Box 1.

Transport is an integral part of trade-enabling infrastructure.

Trade facilitation initiatives often cover at-the-border hard and soft interventions. Hard interventions address physical infrastructure at the border, including border-crossing point (BCP) assets.[3] Soft interventions pay attention to customs efficiency, and develop procedures and digital tools to streamline the movement of goods across borders.

Transport infrastructure, covering roads, railways, air, and sea, assumes importance as beyond the border measure to affect trade (Hummels and Skiba 2004). In addition, enhancement of information technology (IT) connectivity and energy transmission are crucial for smooth operation. Cross-border transport agreement is equally important to ensure smooth movement of vehicles across borders.

---

[2]   The WTO Global Trade Costs Index is based on a new methodology by Egger et al. (2021) that delivers directional trade cost estimates and sector-specific elasticities which are crucial for inferring trade costs from trade-flows data http://tradecosts.wto.org/.

[3]   Examples of BCP assets include parking facilities for cargo vehicles, warehousing facilities, cold storage, testing facilities, banking facilities, electronic weighbridges, etc.

Figure 5: Trade Cost Decomposition
(%)

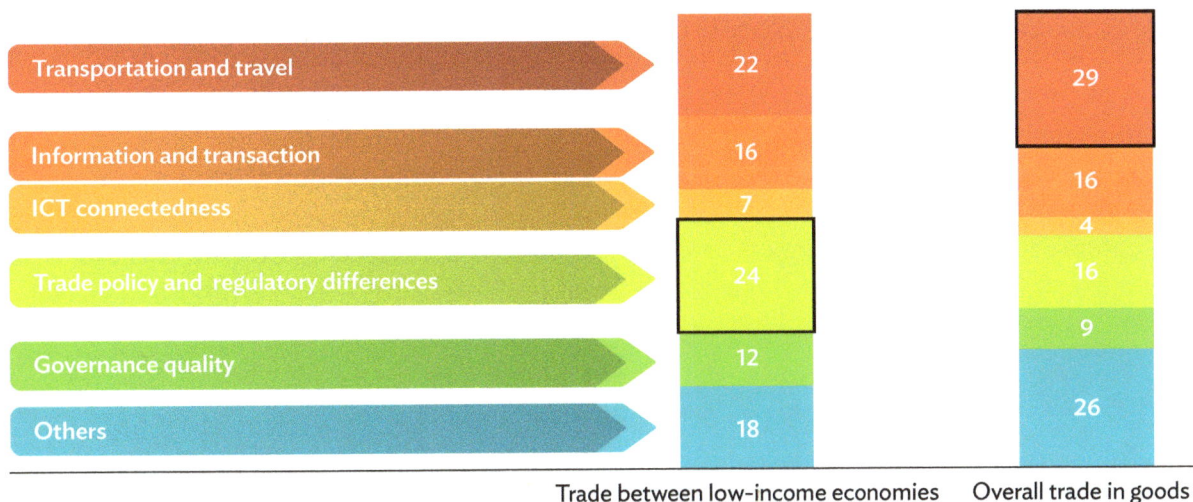

- Transportation and travel
- Information and transaction
- ICT connectedness
- Trade policy and regulatory differences
- Governance quality
- Others

	Trade between low-income economies	Overall trade in goods
Transportation and travel	22	29
Information and transaction	16	16
ICT connectedness	7	4
Trade policy and regulatory differences	24	16
Governance quality	12	9
Others	18	26

ICT = information and communication technology.

Source: World Trade Organization (WTO). 2021. WTO Trade Cost Index: Evolution, Incidence and Determinants. Geneva. https://www.wto.org/english/res_e/reser_e/ersd202106_e.pdf.

Box 1: Key Determinants of Trade Cost Index

1. **Transport and travel cost:** Affected by factors such as cost of freight, time spent in transit (intensity of trade and physical distance between trading partners are inversely related), transport infrastructure, customs procedures, and administrative hurdles.

2. **Information and transaction cost:** Contracting frictions and transaction costs increase with cultural differences and differences in legal systems.

3. **ICT connectedness:** Broad access to competitive information and communication technology (ICT) services improves access to information; lowers transaction and communication cost; and improves efficiency of services that underpin international trade (such as transport, logistics, and finance).

4. **Trade policy and regulatory differences** are the second major component of trade costs in most sectors. Trade restrictive and protectionist policies (for sanitary and phytosanitary technical barriers to trade) barriers act as barriers to trade and increase trade costs. The importance of this component is particularly striking for trade among lower-income economies.

5. **Governance quality:** The quality of institutions has a large, positive effect on international trade and for complex, differentiated goods.

Source: World Trade Organization. 2021. WTO Trade Cost Index: Evolution, Incidence and Determinants. Geneva. http://tradecosts.wto.org/docs/Trade_Cost_Index_Background_Note_24-03-2021.pdf.

Efficiency at the border and beyond the border measures become more relevant for landlocked countries, such as Bhutan, the Lao People's Democratic Republic (Lao PDR), Mongolia, and Nepal, as they rely on trading gateways (seaports) outside the country for imports and exports. For such countries, it is essential to ensure that the cost of transporting goods to the ports in the neighboring countries remains competitive. A case in point is Rwanda, a country in East Africa. Rwanda has developed transport corridors to access ports in neighboring countries, backed with enabling trade agreements. The bulk of Rwanda's exports and imports travel through one of two ports: Mombasa, Kenya (along the "Northern Corridor") or Dar es Salaam, Tanzania (along the "Central Corridor") (Global Business Network Platform n.d.).

Table 6 summarizes context, strategic objectives, and outcomes from selected studies which have emphasized the rationale of an integrated approach for trade enhancement by analyzing trade facilitation and transport together.

Table 6: Summary of Selected Studies on Integrated Approach

Sl. No.	Name of Document	Year	Brief Context to the Report
1	World Bank Group report on *Integration of Transport and Trade Facilitation: Selected Regional Case Studies*	2001	The report analyzes the scope and status of the interrelated processes of trade and transport integration in all five trading blocs: North American Free Trade Agreement, European Union, Mercosur, South Asian Association for Regional Cooperation, and Southern African Development Community. Each trade bloc has been reviewed based on the economic and institutional evolution in the region, presents an economic profile of the component members, and assesses the nature and extent of trade integration. The report provides a case study of Rotterdam Port's ability to retain its efficiency through its twofold approach to trade and transport.
2	Lao People's Democratic Republic (Lao PDR) Trade and Transport Facilitation Assessment (World Bank Group)	2014	The report examines the trade logistics of the Lao PDR. A Trade and Transport Facilitation Assessment was performed using a standardized toolkit and methodology developed by the World Bank to evaluate the quality of the logistics services. The report identifies opportunities for reducing the time and cost for shipping exports and imports between the origin and destination within the Lao PDR and the international gateways such as (i) decreasing the percentage of empty backhauls for container shipments, (ii) introduce transloading infrastructure at the international seaport, (iii) simplifying and automating clearance procedures including electronic data interchange across borders and agencies, (iv) redesigning their supply chains to more efficiently and effectively handle small shipments, and (v) government regulations related to trade finance affect management of cash flow for supply chain participants.
3	The future of trade and transport facilitation: Implications of the WTO Trade Facilitation Agreement (Natural Resources and Infrastructure Division, UNECLAC)	2014	The bulletin analyzes the implications for transport infrastructure services in the UNECLAC region of the future trade facilitation agreement (TFA) concluded under the auspices of the World Trade Organization (WTO). Particular attention is given to the role of transport ministries in facilitating international trade and the concrete obligations and opportunities that will arise with the WTO agreement. The key findings of bulletin are (i) implementation of the TFA, including those of its provisions that do not concern national transport authorities, is likely to improve transport operating costs and times by reducing border-crossing times and/or making them more predictable; (ii) implementation of trade facilitation reforms is likely to enhance returns on investment in transport infrastructure; and (iii) proper implementation of trade facilitation reforms should make shortages and deficiencies of transport infrastructure more noticeable than before, helping governments and the private sector to make a stronger case for investment in transport infrastructure.

continued on next page

Table 6 *continued*

Sl. No.	Name of Document	Year	Brief Context to the Report
4	Trade and Transport Facilitation Monitoring Mechanism in Bangladesh, Bhutan, Nepal: Baseline Study (ADB and UNESCAP)	2017	The report highlights the importance of monitoring trade and transport facilitation from a holistic perspective. The report shows that border-crossing and transport time may account for 1%–2% and 8%–9%, respectively, of total trade time. In light of Bangladesh, Bhutan, India, and Nepal Motor Vehicles Agreement, the report presents both the challenges and enormous opportunities for enhancing transport efficiency along the Bangladesh, Bhutan, India, and Nepal corridors. It identifies that the current average speed of vehicle movement along the corridor is very low and 44%–50% of the transport time could be reduced if the average speed can be improved to 30 kilometers per hour on average. Hence, improving transport and border-crossing infrastructure is one of the key recommendations.

ADB = Asian Development Bank, Mercosur = The Southern Common Market, UNECLAC = United Nations Economic Commission for Latin America and the Caribbean, UNESCAP = United Nations Economic and Social Commission for Asia and the Pacific.
Source: Study team's review.

COVID-19 pandemic trade disruption necessitated an integrated approach with digitalization.

The COVID-19 pandemic led to lockdowns and border closures that restricted movement of goods. Additional protocols (such as requirements for testing, driver swap, trailer swap, or transshipment at warehouses) introduced to ensure the safety of workers, contributed to bottlenecks for freight.[4] Many major ports with a strong gateway function saw their containers throughput plunge in the first half of 2020. Notable examples included Rotterdam (–7%), Shanghai (–6.8%), Los Angeles (–17.1%), Hamburg (–14.7%), Le Havre (–29%), Barcelona (–20.5%), and Valencia (–9.1%). These caused supply chain disruptions creating shortage of goods in consuming economies.

While there was revival of demand in the second half of 2020, translating immediately into increased demand for port services (Cullinane and Haralambides 2021), both port and transport networks were caught unprepared for such a fast transition in demand. As a result, supply chains suffered from shortages in containers, equipment (chassis), truck drivers, and dock labor; the latter due to quarantines and constraints on personal mobility due to COVID-19. Congestion and long turnaround times at and beyond the port continued into 2021.

COVID-19 also highlighted the role of technology as a crisis mitigation tool and resilience-building lever. Ports with smart features generally fared better during the pandemic. Those that invested in digital infrastructure and connectivity and promoted data exchanges among port authorities, shippers, and freight forwarders, navigated the disruptions more smoothly (UNCTAD, 2022a).

Based on the UN global survey on digital and trade facilitation, the COVID-19 pandemic helped accelerate digital transformation, with the implementation of "paperless trade" standing at 64%. However, implementation of "cross-border paperless trade" was significantly low, at 38%,

---

[4]   For example, in the European Union, trucks formed 37-mile-long lines on the A4 highway after Poland closed its border with Germany in mid-March. In India, the lockdown created a shortage of truck drivers, which resulted in over 50,000 containers piling up in the ports of Chennai, Kamajarar, and Kattupalli (IFC 2020).

with bilateral and subregional paperless trade systems implemented either partially or on a pilot basis.[5] Nonetheless, progress in the implementation of paperless trade and cross-border paperless trade measures is remarkable, with increases of 6.3 and 5.4 percentage points, respectively, over the past 2 years. As part of their response to the challenges at borders triggered by the COVID-19 pandemic, many economies made increased use of digital tools to implement measures aimed at increased automation of customs and the digitalization of other regulatory procedures (Figure 6). Examples of such trade facilitation measures include

(i)   establishing specific COVID-19 online information portals,
(ii)   acceptance of digital trade-related documents in place of physical copies (including sanitary and phytosanitary [SPS] certificates), and
(iii)   increase in the number of procedures benefiting from electronic pre-arrival processing.

For example, using the UN Conference on Trade and Development (UNCTAD) Automated System for Customs Data, some countries implemented the use of e-trade permits, paperless processes, and the exemption of taxes to facilitate imports of medical supplies during the pandemic (UNCTAD 2020). These were complementary to the introduction of measures such as "green lanes" (such as in the European Union) or "corridors" for fast clearance of certain products.

Table 7 presents examples of countries which adopted digitized processes to mitigate the disruptive impact of the COVID-19 pandemic and facilitate trade and transport.

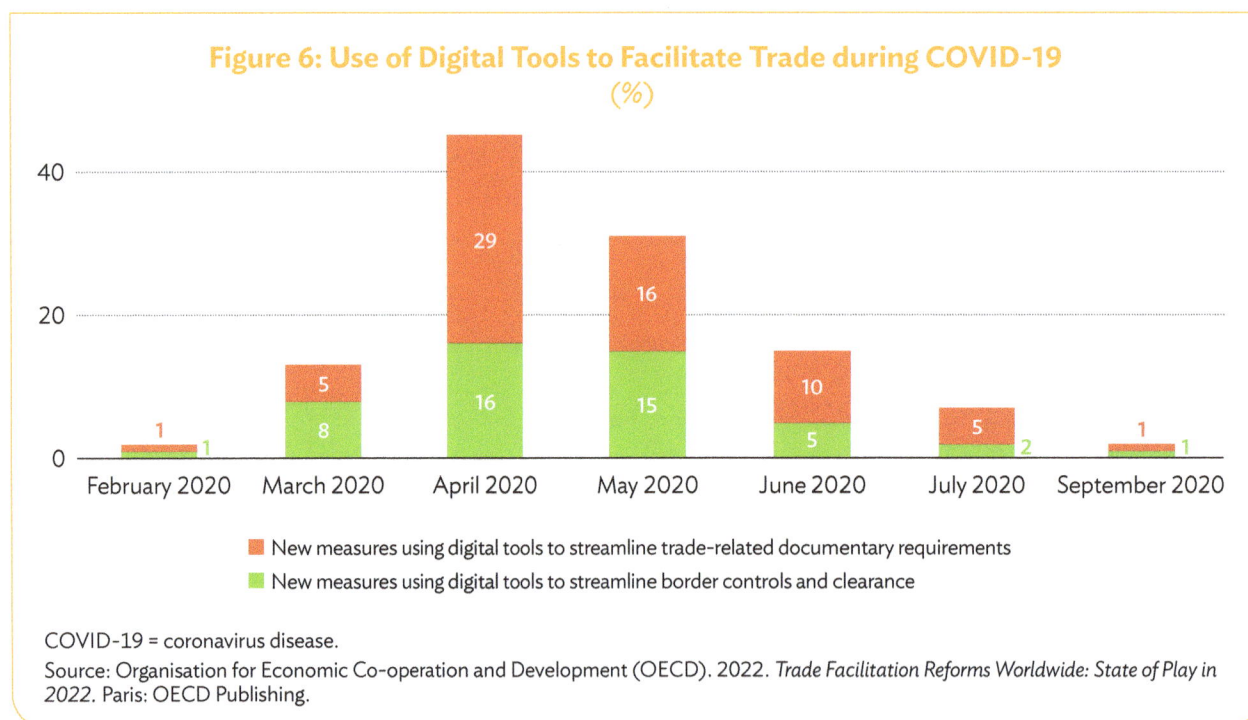

Figure 6: Use of Digital Tools to Facilitate Trade during COVID-19
(%)

COVID-19 = coronavirus disease.
Source: Organisation for Economic Co-operation and Development (OECD). 2022. *Trade Facilitation Reforms Worldwide: State of Play in 2022.* Paris: OECD Publishing.

---

[5]   "Paperless trade" constitutes automated customs systems, internet connection, electronic single window system, electronic submission of customs data, and others. "Cross-border paperless trade" constitutes laws and regulations for electronic transactions, electronic exchange of customs declarations, electronic exchange of certificate of origin, and others.

Table 7: Adoption of Digitization during the COVID-19 Pandemic

Country	Digitization Adopted
Philippines	The Anti-Red Tape Authority, Bureau of Customs, and Food and Drug Administration created the Bayanihan one-stop-shop to import coronavirus disease (COVID-19) critical commodities for commercial distribution.
Mauritius	Customs facilitated free-of-charge, web-based access to the Customs Management System, for electronic submissions and payments, by all economic operators transacting business with customs. This initiative enabled declarants to work from home.
Panama	Paperwork for the import, transshipment, and transit of goods, as well as any customs regime in ports, airports, and land borders, was carried out on the electronic platform of the Integrated Customs Management System.
France	All customs clearance procedures were performed electronically, and the time taken for clearance, except in selection for checking, was down to just a few minutes until goods were released.
Moldova	The certificates of preferential origin of the goods, presented in copies (on paper or electronically), or authenticated with the digital signature (presented in copies or in original), had the same validity as their originals.

Source: World Customs Organization. 2020. What Customs Can do to Mitigate the Effects of the Covid-19 Pandemic: Highlights of WCO Members' Practices 2nd Edition. Brussels. http://www.wcoomd.org/-/media/wco/public/global/pdf/topics/facilitation/activities-and-programmes/natural-disaster/covid_19/covid_19-categorization-of-member-input.pdf?la=en.

While these measures seem to apply only to certain goods, there is an opportunity to embed many of the digital trade facilitation actions permanently, as part of the gradual move to enhanced digitization. Better understanding of the policies that supported the increased use of digital tools in exchanging trade documents can help address existing regulatory challenges in the automation of other documentation requirements.

The aim and structure of the study

This study offers a way to understand trade and transport facilitation in comprehensive manner and provides recommendations to undertake the same at policy-level discussions. It provides an illustrative case study to measure trade readiness of a country at national and subnational (trade corridor) levels. The objective of the study is thus twofold:

- to look at trade and transport facilitation measures in an integrated fashion that is resilient, sustainable, and inclusive; and
- to provide a systematic tool to measure the readiness of a country or trade corridor to enhance international trade.

The approach for this study comprises four workstreams. It includes a secondary review of the existing trade facilitation and transport frameworks of different international organizations across geographies (Workstream-1). Gaps within these guidance documents have been identified in key current and future requirements for enhancement of international trade (Workstream-2). Provisions critical to address these gaps have been identified from global best practices and review of specific literature. Accordingly, a comprehensive list of provisions relevant for trade and transport facilitation has been developed (Workstream-3).

With comprehensive guidance for trade and transport facilitation in place, the study has developed an illustrative framework for assessment of national and subnational readiness through identification of relevant key performance indicators (Workstream-4).

Figure 7 is a schematic diagram of the approach.

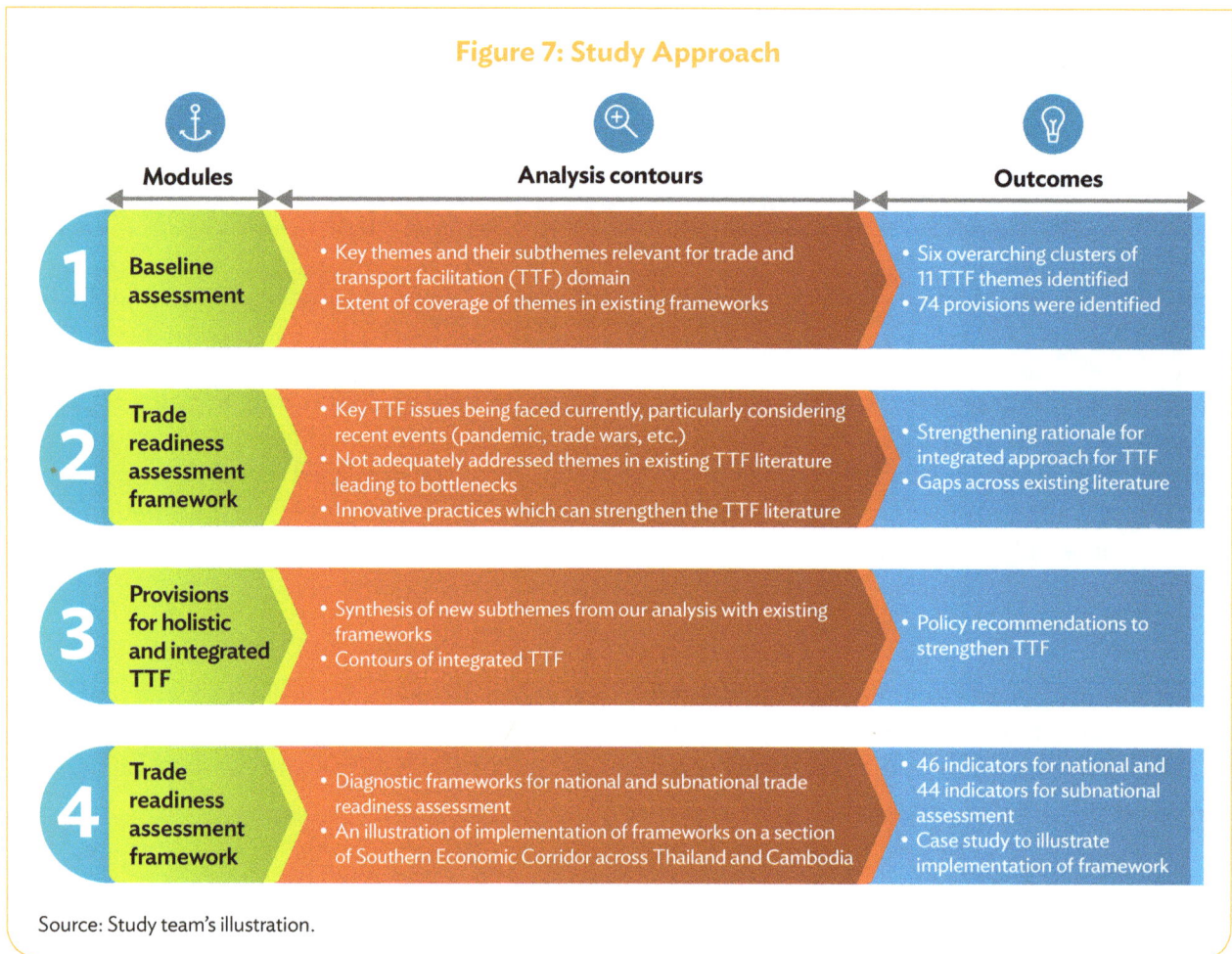

Figure 7: Study Approach

Modules	Analysis contours	Outcomes
1 Baseline assessment	• Key themes and their subthemes relevant for trade and transport facilitation (TTF) domain • Extent of coverage of themes in existing frameworks	• Six overarching clusters of 11 TTF themes identified • 74 provisions were identified
2 Trade readiness assessment framework	• Key TTF issues being faced currently, particularly considering recent events (pandemic, trade wars, etc.) • Not adequately addressed themes in existing TTF literature leading to bottlenecks • Innovative practices which can strengthen the TTF literature	• Strengthening rationale for integrated approach for TTF • Gaps across existing literature
3 Provisions for holistic and integrated TTF	• Synthesis of new subthemes from our analysis with existing frameworks • Contours of integrated TTF	• Policy recommendations to strengthen TTF
4 Trade readiness assessment framework	• Diagnostic frameworks for national and subnational trade readiness assessment • An illustration of implementation of frameworks on a section of Southern Economic Corridor across Thailand and Cambodia	• 46 indicators for national and 44 indicators for subnational assessment • Case study to illustrate implementation of framework

Source: Study team's illustration.

The report is accordingly developed around four chapters. Following the introductory chapter, that includes the need for an integrated approach, the next chapter provides a detailed literature review of the existing framework and policy documents across multiple regions. Chapter 3 provides the policy recommendations for pursuing a comprehensive approach of soft and hard infrastructure to enhance international trade. This builds on the existing measures and the gaps identified in the report. The last chapter (Chapter 4) presents a case study employing the enhanced framework and measuring trade readiness in terms of infrastructure at national and subnational (trade corridor) levels.

2. Current State of Trade and Transport Facilitation

2.1 Constituents of Trade and Transport Facilitation across Existing Documents

Key themes of trade and transport facilitation

As discussed in Chapter 1, high tariffs were the principal policy-based barriers to trade to be overcome in the early years of pursuing trade facilitation. These barriers were mitigated to a large extent through measures such as the General Agreement on Tariffs and Trade 1947/World Trade Organization 1995, regional free trade agreements, etc. Important policy obstacles to address now revolve around the concept of trade facilitation, both in its traditional sense as related to customs procedures at borders, and addressing the constraints of physical infrastructure and inclusive and sustainable growth (Staples and Harris 2009).

Various international and regional guiding documents and agreements have been analyzed to develop understanding of the themes under the existing guiding documents. The provisions are the strategic action points required to be implemented under the documents. The themes are topics with a specific trade and transport facilitation objective. Clusters for the scope of this report are groups of themes with broader conceptual overlap.

The report considers multilateral and selected regional and subregional regional cooperation mechanisms with commitments in trade and transport facilitation:

(i)   WTO Trade Facilitation Agreement,
(ii)   ADB–South Asia Subregional Economic Cooperation (SASEC) Operational Plan 2016–25,
(iii)   ADB–Central Asia Regional Economic Cooperation (CAREC) Integrated Trade Agenda 2030,
(iv)   ASEAN Trade Facilitation Framework,
(v)   ADB–UNESCAP Regional Cooperation for Trade and Transport Connectivity in the Age of the Pandemic,
(vi)   UN Global Survey on Digital and Sustainable Trade Facilitation,
(vii)   World Bank Trade and Transport Facilitation Assessment Framework, and
(viii) ADB GMS Trade and Transport Facilitation – Action Program.

All ADB-led subregional initiatives are considered, while multilateral and other framework and guideline documents prepared by international organizations are covered by the discussion to strengthen the findings. Appendix 1 briefly describes trade facilitation commitments in each of the cooperation agendas considered in this study.

Based on these cooperation documents, the study divides the provisions covered under each of these under themes and clusters. The study consolidates 97 provisions under 11 themes and 6 clusters, as discussed below.

Trade and transport facilitation provisions are classified across six clusters of themes.

The study mapped the guiding documents and their priority areas and provisions to analyze the areas covered in these frameworks. The study identified 11 themes covered by trade and transport facilitation and on further analysis, the six clusters, by clubbing similar themes together (Figure 8).

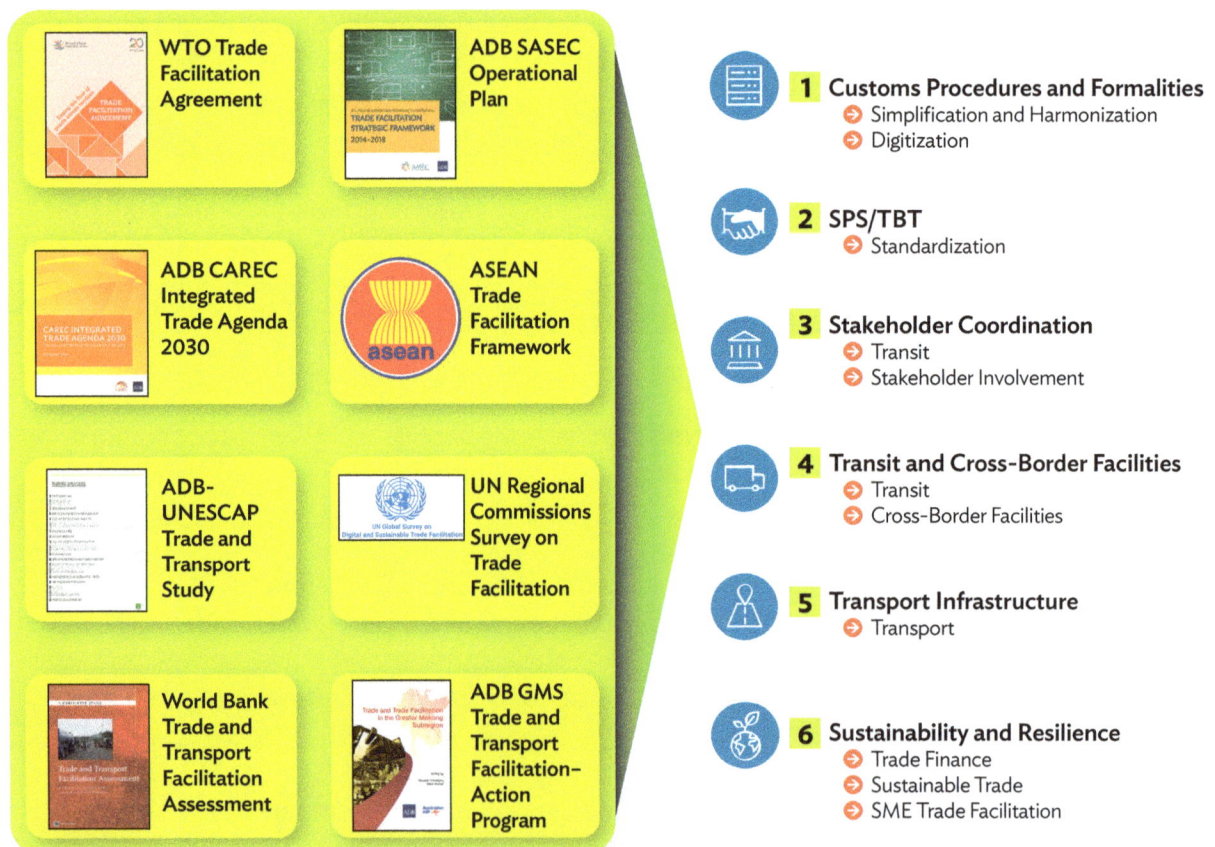

Figure 8: Themes across Trade and Transport Facilitation Guiding Documents

ADB = Asian Development Bank, ASEAN = Association of Southeast Asian Nations, CAREC = Central Asia Regional Economic Cooperation Program, GMS = Greater Mekong Subregion, SASEC = South Asia Subregional Economic Cooperation, SME = small and medium-sized enterprise, SPS/TBT = sanitary and phytosanitary measures/technical barriers to trade UN = United Nations, UNESCAP = UN Economic and Social Commission for Asia and the Pacific, WTO = World Trade Organization.
Source: Study team's illustration.

The thematic clusters and their components are (with provisions of all listed in Appendix 2 Table A.1 to Table A.11):

(i) **Customs Procedures and Formalities:** This cluster consists of two themes: Simplification and Harmonization, and Digitization. The Simplification and Harmonization theme lists 19 provisions that aim to tackle "soft" challenges or nontariff barriers to trade by enhancing transparency and accessibility of trade related measures, simplification of processes, minimization/elimination of unnecessary or restrictive trade practices, updating rules and regulations based on adoption of modern technology, etc.

The Digitization theme covers digitization of trade processes and portals and includes provisions such as automation of customs management systems, development and deployment of national single windows, adoption of electronic documentation where possible, and facilitating electronic financial transactions. The cluster also includes digital infrastructure such as customs management systems, single windows, etc.

(ii) **Sanitary and Phytosanitary Measures/Technical Barriers to Trade:** These include technical barriers to trade in international standardization, testing laboratories, SPS regulations and measures, etc. The cluster includes provisions on strengthening competencies of testing labs to comply with SPS measures, establishing national standards, strengthening national conformance assessment boards, etc.

(iii) **Stakeholder Coordination:** The cluster's two components are Institutional Coordination/ Capacity Building and Stakeholder Involvement. Institutional coordination relates to organizational framework for efficiently managing trade-related activities and coordinating with other border agencies both domestic and international to fulfill their directive. The theme includes measures on cooperation and coordination between different customs and government agencies, operational and skill improvement measures, adoption of and upgrade of technologies, alignment of formalities with the neighboring countries, etc. The second theme, Stakeholder Involvement, facilitates and promotes effective mechanisms for consultations and discussions with relevant public and private stakeholders while formulating, implementing, or reviewing rules and procedures related to trade and transport facilitation.

(iv) **Transit and Cross-Border Facilities:** The cluster's two themes are Transit and Cross-Border Facilities. The transit theme refers to provisions enabling seamless movement of goods across countries participating in trade or transit. These provisions simplify and streamline procedures at border-crossing. The Cross-Border Facilities theme covers various facilities necessary at border-crossing points and includes hard infrastructure like green lanes, parking places, storage, testing laboratories, social amenities, etc.

(v) **Transport Infrastructure:** This cluster covers the hard infrastructure facilitating transport connectivity across the trade value chain and includes multimodal transport, logistics infrastructure, and the governing policies and regulations.

(vi) **Sustainability and Resilience:** The cluster contains provisions that facilitate inclusive and sustainable growth, build resilience into the global supply chain system, and mitigate global trade disruptions caused by events like the COVID-19 pandemic or the Russian invasion of Ukraine. The cluster includes three themes: Trade Finance, SME Trade Facilitation, and Sustainable Trade. Trade finance plays an increasing role in facilitating trade flows. This theme includes provisions on accessibility to trade finance, variety of trade finance services, inclusion of trade finance in single window portals, etc. The second theme, SME Trade Facilitation, contains trade facilitation measures boosting their competitiveness and participation in global trade and achieving inclusive growth. The provisions include ensuring representation of small and medium-sized enterprises (SMEs) in the National Trade Facilitation Commitee (NTFC), easing access to trade finance, enabling single window access, etc.[6] The Sustainable Trade theme includes trade facilitation provisions pertaining to gender inequalities, environmental impact of trade and transport, and emergency measures and protocols.

Trade and transport facilitation priorities in guiding documents have evolved.

International and regional trade facilitation frameworks have evolved. Initially, the focus was on procedural and regulatory aspects of trade to simplify complex procedures, reengineer trade documentation processes, develop and implement international standards, etc. These were gradually broadened to include transparency, standardization of trade documents, coordination between border agencies and the private sector, etc. The regional trade agreements have also evolved to include provisions on international standards, and WTO TFA measures such as transit provisions, advance rulings, cooperation and exchange of information, risk management, single window and automation, etc. (UNCTAD 2011) Increasingly, it has been realized that trade barriers and the enablers of trade such as infrastructural aspects should be covered simultaneously and holistically.

More recent trade facilitation frameworks and studies talk about building sustainable trade, focusing on facilitating trade finance, measures for SMEs and women-driven firms, and provisions to mitigate the impact of unforeseen crises. Figure 9 shows the evolving focus of key trade and transport facilitation documents.

The WTO TFA, finalized in 2013, contains rules covering import, export, and transit formalities and procedures. It provided guidance for enhancing trade through facilitating "soft" aspects. These included customs procedures and formalities, standardization measures, digitization of trade practices, and institutional coordination. Over time, as the need for scaling physical infrastructure to meet the growing demands of increasing trade was realized, the newer trade and transport facilitation documents expanded focus to additional aspects of trade facilitation over and above the procedural soft challenges.

---

[6] The NTFCs were created as part of the WTO TFA when it entered into force with the aim of becoming coordinators of trade facilitation reforms at the national level. The committee's institutional arrangements and responsibilities can be found in Article 23 of the TFA. Sections 3.2.3 and 3.2.4 detail the role of the institution.

Figure 9: Evolving Focus in Trade Facilitation

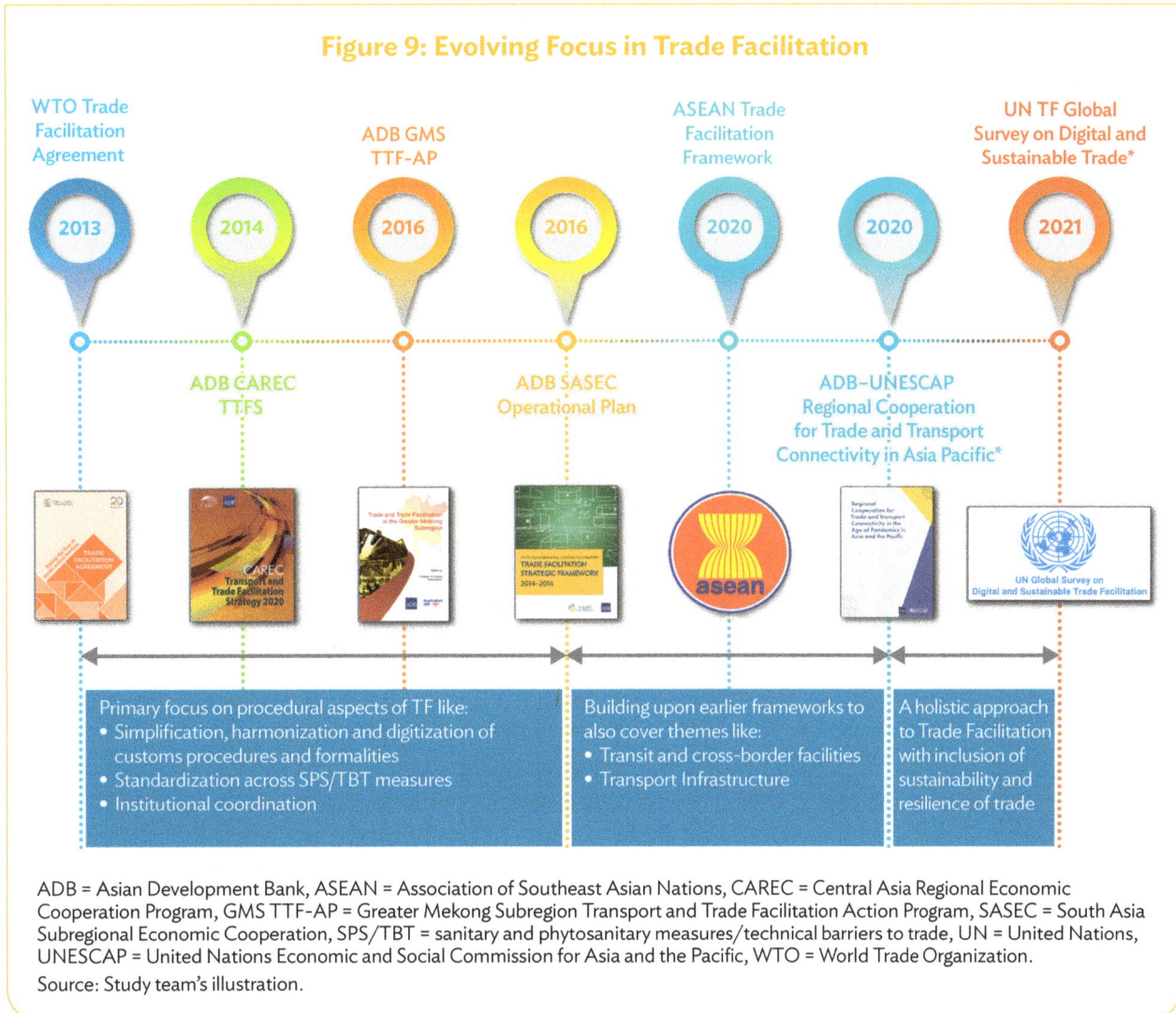

WTO Trade Facilitation Agreement — **2013**

ADB GMS TTF-AP — **2014**

2016

2016

ASEAN Trade Facilitation Framework — **2020**

2020

UN TF Global Survey on Digital and Sustainable Trade* — **2021**

ADB CAREC TTFS

ADB SASEC Operational Plan

ADB–UNESCAP Regional Cooperation for Trade and Transport Connectivity in Asia Pacific*

Primary focus on procedural aspects of TF like:
- Simplification, harmonization and digitization of customs procedures and formalities
- Standardization across SPS/TBT measures
- Institutional coordination

Building upon earlier frameworks to also cover themes like:
- Transit and cross-border facilities
- Transport Infrastructure

A holistic approach to Trade Facilitation with inclusion of sustainability and resilience of trade

ADB = Asian Development Bank, ASEAN = Association of Southeast Asian Nations, CAREC = Central Asia Regional Economic Cooperation Program, GMS TTF-AP = Greater Mekong Subregion Transport and Trade Facilitation Action Program, SASEC = South Asia Subregional Economic Cooperation, SPS/TBT = sanitary and phytosanitary measures/technical barriers to trade, UN = United Nations, UNESCAP = United Nations Economic and Social Commission for Asia and the Pacific, WTO = World Trade Organization.
Source: Study team's illustration.

Trade facilitation frameworks such as the SASEC Operational Plan, GMS Transport and Trade Facilitation Action Program and CAREC Transport and Trade Facilitation Strategy included within their scope, development of transit agreements and cross-border facilities, development of transport infrastructure, and streamlining of the regulations governing the logistics services. Transit agreements complement these frameworks in their trade facilitation measures with exchange of traffic rights, freedom of transit, etc. These frameworks talk extensively about development of multimodal transport infrastructure to cater to the efficient movement of goods. Development of cross-border facilities was encouraged to facilitate efficient handling of cargo at the border-crossing points and reducing overall processing and clearing times.

In recent years, focus on inclusive growth has increased while trade facilitation frameworks have included digital and sustainable trade with focus on paperless trade, mitigating the impact of gender disparity, inclusive growth of SMEs, and improving access to trade finance. The recent Global Survey on Digital and Sustainable Trade facilitation includes these aspects and also recognizes the need for trade facilitation measures in times of crisis. This need is evident in the challenges posed by the COVID-19 pandemic on the global supply chain.

With the overall focus largely on improving operational efficiency in trade, trade facilitation seems to lack focus on mitigating climate change consequences. Limited literature is available that discusses the impact of trade on greenhouse gas emissions. Trade facilitation could be a powerful tool to address these consequences by promoting climate-friendly technologies to reduce nontariff barriers. Shifting to paperless trade—using only ICT, electronic data, and documents in trade transactions for a complete end-to-end solution to comply with trade regulations and procedures—has the potential to eliminate 13 million tons of carbon dioxide (CO_2) emissions per year for the Asia and Pacific region (UNESCAP and UNCTAD 2021).

Emphasis on trade and transport facilitation themes varies across guiding frameworks.

As discussed in the previous section, trade and transport facilitation comprises six clusters with 11 themes based on review of some of the major frameworks and guidance documents. The study mapped the coverage of identified trade and transport facilitation themes across frameworks and other guidance documents under review. Table 8 illustrates mapping done for Simplification and Harmonization, with 19 provisions mapped across the reviewed frameworks and guidance documents. While provisions of risk management systems and authorized economic operators are covered by seven of eight reviewed frameworks and documents, provisions such as nondiscriminatory rules and procedures, adequate access to legal procedures, and 24/7 clearance systems at major ports are present across only a few of the documents. As can be seen from the table, the WTO TFA and the UN survey both comparatively address the issue most extensively among the reviewed frameworks. Similar mapping for the rest of the clusters and their themes have been placed in Appendix 2.

A summary of this mapping exercise has been shown in Table 9. It highlights the extent of coverage of themes and clusters across various trade and transport facilitation documents. For a particular theme, the trade and transport facilitation document with highest relative coverage has been indicated through a 100%-solid Harvey ball and progressive reduction in coverage is depicted through corresponding hollowness of the Harvey ball. For example, WTO TFA covers the Simplification and Harmonization theme in relatively maximum depth. So, it has been indicated with a 100%-solid Harvey ball and other frameworks and guidance documents have been indicated with relatively hollower Harvey balls denoting lesser coverage.

We have also aggregated coverage of these provisions at the level of clusters and themes. It has helped us in categorizing clusters and themes according to their coverage across trade and transport facilitation documents under review in terms of high, medium, and low. For example, themes such as Simplification and Harmonization, Digitization, Standardization, Institutional Coordination/Capacity Building, and Transit are covered across most of the frameworks and documents and hence marked with "high" coverage, while themes such as Transport Infrastructure, SME Trade Facilitation, and Sustainable Trade are covered in fewer frameworks and hence marked with low coverage.

Table 8: Coverage of Simplification and Harmonization Provisions across Guiding Documents

	Simplification and Harmonization	WTO TFA	ADB SASEC	CAREC CITA 2030	ASEAN	ADB-UNESCAP	UNTF Survey	World Bank	ADB GMS
1	Accede to the Revised Kyoto Convention		✓	✓	✓				✓
2	Implement the WCO Safe Framework		✓	✓					
3	Reengineer Business Processes and Documentation to Promote Efficiencies		✓						
4	Adoption of New Simplified Customs Codes That are Harmonized with International Standards.	✓		✓	✓				✓
5	Strengthen Risk Management Systems at BCPs in Order to Expedite the Clearance	✓	✓	✓	✓	✓	✓	✓	✓
6	Simplify Trade Rules and Procedures, Remove or Reduce Restrictive or Unnecessary Practices	✓		✓	✓	✓		✓	
7	Make Rules and Procedures Nondiscriminatory in Nature	✓			✓				
8	Facilitate Access to Adequate Legal Appeal Procedures	✓			✓		✓		
9	Creating an Outreach Portal (e.g., Single-Window COVID-19 Portal) to Disseminate Information					✓	✓		
10	Publishing and Notifying Trade Facilitation Measures to Relevant International Organizations					✓			
11	Create 24/7 Clearance System at Major Trade Gateways					✓			
12	Development of Special Provisions (e.g., Reduction and Waiving of Taxes and Duties) for Trade of Essential Goods During Emergencies					✓			
13	Allowing Trusted Traders/Authorized Economic Operators with Expedited Clearance	✓	✓	✓	✓	✓	✓		✓
14	Publication of Existing Import–Export Regulations on the Internet	✓			✓		✓		
15	Advance Publication/Notification of New Trade-Related Regulations before their Implementation	✓					✓		
16	Advance Ruling on Tariff Classification and Origin of Imported Goods	✓			✓		✓		✓
17	Adoption of Post-Clearance Audit Procedures	✓		✓	✓		✓		
18	Establishment and Publication of Average Release Times	✓			✓		✓		✓
19	Online Publication of Emergency Trade Facilitation Measures						✓		

ADB = Asian Development Bank, ASEAN = Association of Southeast Asian Nations, BCPs = border-crossing point, CAREC = Central Asia Regional Economic Cooperation, CITA = CAREC Integrated Trade Agenda, COVID-19 = coronavirus disease, GMS = Greater Mekong Subregion, SASEC = South Asia Subregional Economic Cooperation, UNESCAP = United Nations Economic and Social Commission for Asia and the Pacific, UN TF = United Nations Trade Facilitation, WCO = World Customs Organization, WTO TFA = World Trade Organization Trade Facilitation Agreement.

Sources: Data from the reviewed trade facilitation frameworks and guiding documents such as the WTO TFA, SASEC Operational Plan, CITA 2030, etc., and study team's estimates.

Table 9: Topic Coverage across Trade and Transport Facilitation Frameworks

Relative Coverage of Thematic Clusters across TTF Frameworks			WTO TFA	SASEC OP 2016–2025	CAREC CITA 2030	ASEAN TTF	ADB–ESCAP Study	UN TF Survey	WB TTFA	GMS TTF–AP
Customs Procedures and Formalities		Simplification and Harmonization	●	◐	◐	◐	◐	◐	◐	◔
		Digitization	◐	◔	◕	◐	◐	●	◐	◔
SPS/TBT		Standardization	◐	●	◐	◐	◐	●	○	◔
Stakeholder Coordination		Institutional Coordination/ Capacity Building	●	◔	◐	○	◐	◔	◔	◕
		Stakeholder Involvement	●	○	◐	●	◐	◐	◕	○
Transit and Cross-Border Facilities		Transit	◐	◔	◐	◔	◐	●	○	●
		Cross-border Facilities	○	●	◐	○	○	○	◔	◔
Transport		Transport Infrastructure	○	○	○	○	○	○	●	○
		Trade Finance	○	○	◔	◔	◐	●	◕	○
Sustainability and Resilience		SME Trade Facilitation	○	○	◔	○	◔	●	○	○
		Sustainable Trade	○	○	○	○	○	●	○	○

● —Maximum coverage to least coverage ➤ ○, * = Survey, ▨ High coverage , ▨ Medium coverage , ▨ Low coverage .

ADB = Asian Development Bank, ASEAN = Association of Southeast Asian Nations, CAREC = Central Asia Regional Economic Cooperation, CITA = CAREC Integrated Trade Agenda, GMS TTF-AP = Greater Mekong Subregion Transport and Trade Facilitation Action Program, SASEC OP = South Asia Subregional Economic Cooperation Operational Plan, SME = small and medium-sized enterprise, SPS/TBT = sanitary and phytosanitary/technical barriers to trade, UNESCAP = United Nations Economic and Social Commission for Asia and the Pacific, UN TF = United Nations Trade Facilitation, WB TTFA = World Bank Transport and Trade Facilitation Assessment, WTO TFA = World Trade Organization Trade Facilitation Agreement, TTF = transport and trade facilitation.

Source: Data from various guiding frameworks and documents including the WTO TFA, ADB SASEC OP, ADB CAREC Integrated Trade Agenda, GMS TTF, etc., WB TTFA, UN Digital and Sustainable Trade Facilitation: Global Report 2021, etc. and study team's estimates.

Hard infrastructure elements such as Cross-Border Facilities and soft aspects such as Stakeholder Involvement and Trade Finance themes are covered in about half of the reviewed frameworks and hence marked as medium coverage thematic areas.

2.2 Analysis of Key Transport Agreements and Transport Conventions

Overview of key transport agreements

Transport agreements also form a key part of the trade and transport facilitation process and contribute to ease of transit, better transport infrastructure, and coordinated customs operations at frontier posts, etc. This section reviews selected key bilateral and multilateral transport agreements and their provisions. The transport agreements studied comprise articles on either or all of road, rail, and maritime transport. Table 10 briefly reviews the provisions contained in the respective agreements.

Table 10: Summary of Provisions in Transport Agreements

Sr. No.	Agreement	Provisions
1	ASEAN Framework Agreement on Facilitation of Inter-State Transport	The agreement contains provisions to facilitate inter-state transport of goods between and among Association of Southeast Asian Nations (ASEAN) member states. The agreement contains provisions that grant the right to inter-state transport, designation of transport routes and frontier posts, regulations and procedures for road transport, customs control, and SPS measures and institutional arrangements.
2	COMESA-EAC-SADC Tripartite Multilateral Cross-Border Road Transport Agreement	Tripartite legal framework for harmonization of road traffic and transport-related aspects, including vehicle registration documents, transport operator registration, vehicle fitness testing, driver training and testing, as well as driving license categories based on appropriate international standards, including United Nations standards.
3	Economic Cooperation Organization Transit Transport Agreement	The agreement contains provisions for transit vehicles to be exempt from customs duties, taxes, etc., roads, railways, and internal waterways to be constructed and maintained as per characteristics set out in the agreement. It encourages and promotes multimodal transport, directs to maintain adequate facilities for transport and transit, measures to expedite transit clearance, measures for safety and regulation of traffic, permits, technical requirement for vehicles, simplification and harmonization of customs procedures, etc.
4	Intergovernmental Agreement on Asian Highway Network	Provides framework for coordinated development of international highways in Asia as well as between Asia and Europe, improving quality of infrastructure and efficiency of operation. The roads, route signs, etc. in the Asian highway network should be brought into conformity with Asian highway design standards.
5	Motor Vehicles Agreement between Bangladesh, Bhutan, India, and Nepal	The agreement contains provisions for regulation of passenger, personal, and cargo vehicular traffic between Bangladesh, Bhutan, India, and Nepal. The provisions include the granting of traffic rights for vehicles, provisions for travel permits, list of documents, fees and charges, road safety and signage, business facilitation, implementation mechanism, etc.

continued on next page

Table 10 *continued*

Sr. No.	Agreement	Provisions
6	**Multilateral Agreement on International Transport for Development of the Europe–the Caucasus–Asia corridor**	The agreement contains the provisions to grant the rights of transit of international means of transport, ensure the most effective arrangements for facilitation of transport, exemption from taxes, duties and other payments for transport in transit, measures to ensure safety of traffic, passengers and carriers, security of goods and means of transport, as well as protection of the environment.
7	**Bilateral Road Transport Agreement between South Africa and Zimbabwe, Malawi, Zambia, and Mozambique**	The agreement is limited to bilateral trade and vehicle movement. It contains the procedures for application of permit for a carrier for transit, provisions for vehicle manifest, vehicular requirements and documentation, harmonization of standards, for vehicles and drivers, etc.
8	**India–Bangladesh Agreement on Coastal Shipping**	The agreement contains provisions for same treatment to each other's vessels as it would have done to national vessels used in international shipping. The trade would be treated as coastal shipping, eligible for 40% concession on vessel and cargo charges. The agreement would help reduce congestion at the Petrapole–Benapole Land Customs Station.[a]

ASEAN = Association of Southeast Asian Nations, COMESA-EAC-SADC = Common Market for Eastern and Southern Africa; the East Africa Community and the Southern African Development Community, SPS = sanitary and phytosanitary.

[a] The Land Customs Station is a terminology used on the Indian subcontinent to define large facilities providing transit, customs and immigration, and cargo handling services for goods and passengers between neighboring countries.

Source: Study team's estimates

The agreements facilitate the grant of the transit rights to the vehicles of contracting parties in the territories of the other contracting party/parties. The articles in the agreement contain provisions on the transport operations, registration for permits, standards of infrastructure, control measures, exemption from additional duties and taxes, implementation mechanism and framework, etc. Table 11 presents a comparative analysis of the reviewed key transport agreements. There are 13 key areas on which the provisions are based on these transport agreements (Table 11). While the Economic Cooperation Organization Transit Transport Agreement is the most comprehensive agreement containing provisions on road, rail, and maritime transport denoted by the 100%-full Harvey ball, the Asian Highway network agreement is the least comprehensive one covering the standards and quality of road transport infrastructure denoted by the hollow Harvey ball.

Overview of the key transport conventions

We also have conducted a brief study of six key transport conventions as briefed in Table 12. Transport conventions provide a uniform and harmonized set of rules for contracting parties, which enables them to create an environment of efficient, low-cost, and seamless cross-border trade. For example, the Transports Internationaux Routiers (TIR) convention aims at establishing an international customs transit system, harmonization of frontier control of goods, and mutual recognition of customs control across contracting parties, which has led to increased trade volumes and establishment of intelligent borders (enhanced cross-border cooperation, increased revenues, and secure and effective border controls).

Table 11: Comparative Coverage in Transport Agreements

Agreements\Provisions	Coverage	Harmonized Traffic Regulations	Designated Transport Routes	Transport Infrastructure Standards	Facilities at Frontier Posts	Technical Requirements	Mutual Recognition of Documents	Issuance of Visa for Operators	Assistance in Case of Accidents	Permit Requirement	Fees and Charges	Temporary Admission	Road Safety and Signs	Border Coordination
ASEAN Framework Agreement on Facilitation of Inter-State Transport	◗	✓	✓		✓	✓	✓	✓	✓	✓	✓	✓	✓	✓
Multilateral Cross-Border Road Transport Agreement	◔					✓				✓	✓	✓		
ECO Transit Transport Agreement	●	✓	✓	✓	✓	✓	✓	✓	✓	✓	✓	✓	✓	✓
Asian Highway Network	○		✓	✓									✓	
BBIN Motor Vehicles Agreement	◑	✓	✓		✓	✓	✓	✓	✓	✓	✓	✓	✓	✓
Multilateral Agreement on International Transport for Development of the Europe– the Caucasus–Asia corridor	◑						✓	✓		✓		✓	✓	✓
Bilateral Road Transport Agreement between South Africa and Zimbabwe, Malawi, Zambia, and Mozambique	◑				✓	✓	✓		✓	✓	✓	✓		✓
India–Bangladesh Agreement on Coastal Shipping	◑	—	—	—	✓	✓	✓			✓	✓	✓	—	✓

— = Not applicable; ASEAN = Association of Southeast Asian Nations; BBIN = Bangladesh, Bhutan, India, Nepal; ECO = Economic Cooperation Organization.
Source: Study team's estimates.

However, despite the advantages, uniform implementation of conventions across countries has emerged as a challenge, since it depends on a minimum required ratification by countries to come into force (only three of six conventions discussed below are currently in force). Additionally, international transport issues are too varied to be realistically addressed within the framework of a single convention or protocol. Hence, countries become unwilling to accept the terms of a convention that normally has a generalized form of rules and does not cater to localized technical and governance scenario of a country or subnational region.

Table 12: Summary of Key Transport Conventions

Name of Convention	Status	Scope of Application	Key Features
United Nations Conference on a Convention on International Multimodal Transport, 1980	Convention not yet in force, the required number of parties for its entry into force is 30, while the actual number of signatory parties is 11[a]	The provisions of this convention shall apply to all contracts of multimodal transport (MMT) (at least two modes of transport) between places in two contracting states (place of taking charge of goods and place of delivery)	➡ The convention facilitates the orderly expansion of world trade by determining rules relating to the carriage of goods by international multimodal transport documents (negotiable/non-negotiable) to be issued by the MMT operator or by somebody with delegated authority. The multimodal document is the prima facie evidence of the taking in charge by the MMT operator of the goods as described therein ➡ When the MMT operator is liable for loss resulting from damage to the goods, its liability shall be limited to an amount not exceeding 920 units of account per package or other shipping unit, or 2.75 units of account per kilogram of gross weight of the goods lost or damaged, whichever is the higher ➡ In case of delay of goods delivery, liability will be limited to an amount equivalent to 2.5 times the freight payable for the goods delayed, but not exceeding the total freight payable under the MMT contract. The limits of liability provided for in this convention shall apply in any action against the MMT operator in respect of loss resulting from loss of or damage to the goods, as well as from delay in delivery, whether the action be founded in contract or not
Customs Convention on the International Transport of Goods Under Cover of TIR Carnets (The TIR Convention), 1975	Convention in force with 77 signatory parties	The convention applies to the transport of goods without intermediate reloading, in road vehicles, combination of vehicles, or in containers across one or more frontiers between custom office of departure and destination of contracting parties	➡ The TIR Convention offers the legal, procedural and operational framework for transit by the issue of TIR Carnet (guarantee document) either in the country of departure or in the country in which the holder is established or resident by a guaranteeing association ➡ Each contracting party may authorize associations to issue TIR Carnets and to act as guarantors ➡ The guaranteeing association shall undertake to pay the import or export duties and taxes, together with any default interest, due under the customs laws and regulations in which any irregularity has been noted ➡ The TIR Carnet has a time limit as specified by the issuing association and is valid until the completion of the TIR operation. Unless otherwise authorized, the total number of customs offices of departure and destination may not exceed four

continued on next page

Table 12 *continued*

Name of Convention	Status	Scope of Application	Key Features
The Convention on the Contract for the International Carriage of Goods by Road, 1956	Convention in force with 58 signatory parties	The convention applies to every contract for goods carriage by road, where the place of departure and delivery are situated in two different countries, where at least one is a contracting country	● The contract of carriage shall be confirmed by the making of a consignment note which is the prima facie evidence of the carriage of goods ● The sender shall be responsible for all expenses for damage sustained by the carrier by reason of the inaccuracy or inadequacy in the consignment note. The sender shall be liable to the carrier for any damage caused by the absence, inadequacy, or irregularity of customs documents ● The carrier shall be liable for the total or partial loss of the goods and for damage thereto occurring between the time when it takes over the goods and the time of delivery, as well as for any delay in delivery (compensation will not exceed 25 francs per kilogram of gross weight) ● If carriage governed by a single contract is performed by successive road carriers, each of them shall be responsible for the performance of the whole operation
United Nations Convention on Contracts for the International Carriage of Goods Wholly or Partly by Sea, (Rotterdam Rules) 2009	Convention not yet in force (requirement of 20 signatory parties), currently five signatory parties	The convention applies to contracts of carriage in which any one of the places—place of receipt, place of delivery, port of loading, or port of discharge—are located in a contracting state	● The convention provides mandatory standards of liability for loss or damage arising from the international carriage of goods by sea that may involve other modes of transport, and is intended to provide a modern successor to earlier international conventions in the field: the so-called Hague Rules 1924, the Hague-Visby Rules 1968, and the Hamburg Rules 1978 (ratification for this convention will require the denouncement of the other conventions) ● The convention supports electronic transport documents (negotiable and non-negotiable) in addition to traditional transport documents to be provided by the carrier (signed by the carrier or an authority on carrier's behalf). ● The compensation payable by the carrier for the loss and damage of goods is calculated by reference to the value of such goods (fixed according to the commodity exchange price/market price/normal value of the goods of same kind and quality) at the place and time of delivery. The carrier is not liable to any other payment except when the carrier and shipper have decided to calculate in a different manner (liability on the carrier will be removed if the goods were destroyed in lieu of saving lives)

continued on next page

Table 12 *continued*

Name of Convention	Status	Scope of Application	Key Features
Convention on International Customs Transit Procedures for the Carriage of Goods by Rail under Cover of SMGS Consignment Notes, 2006	Convention not yet in force, (requirement of five signatory parties), currently there is one signatory party	This Convention shall apply to the carriage of goods under cover of a Consignment Note accepted by each Contracting Party and used in accordance with the provisions of this Convention as a Customs transit document.	● A Consignment Note used in accordance with this convention and identification measures taken by the competent authorities of a contracting party shall have the same legal effect in the other contracting parties as a consignment note used in accordance with the rules and identification measures taken by each contracting party's own competent authorities. ● Provision for mutual assistance for sharing of all available information in the form of documents, reports, etc. between the competent authorities of the contracting parties ● The railway companies (railways) of the contracting parties shall be jointly and severally responsible for the proper conduct of international customs transit operations entering the territories of the said contracting parties. ● The railway companies shall be liable for any customs payments, which may become due as a result of an infringement or irregularity committed in the course of or in connection with the underlying transit operation (except in case of accidents)
International Convention to Facilitate the Crossing of Frontiers for Goods Carried by Rail, 1952	Convention in force with 12 signatory parties	This convention is applicable to railway carrying line of contracting parties	● Provision for joint examination by contracting parties to designate a station for carrying out examinations required under the legislation of the two countries. Where the establishment of such stations for two-way traffic examinations is found to be impracticable, the contracting parties shall jointly examine the possibility of making suitable arrangement ● Any equipment required for the functioning of the services of the adjoining country shall be imported on a temporary basis and re-exported free of all customs duties.

TIR = Transports Internationaux Routiers.

[a] No new accessions since 1996.

Sources: United Nations (UN). 1981. United Nations Conference on a Convention on International Multimodal Transport. https://unctad.org/system/files/official-document/tdmtconf17_en.pdf, UN. 1975. Customs Convention on the International Transport of Goods under Cover of TIR Carnets (TIR Convention). https://unece.org/DAM/tir/handbook/TIRConventionENFRRU.pdf , UN. 1956. Convention on the Contract for the International Carriage of Goods by Road. https://unece.org/DAM/trans/conventn/cmr_e.pdf, UN. 2009. United Nations Convention on Contracts for the International Carriage of Goods Wholly or Partly by Sea. https://uncitral.un.org/sites/uncitral.un.org/files/media-documents/uncitral/en/rotterdam-rules-e.pdf, UN. 2006. Convention on International Customs Transit Procedures for the Carriage of Goods by Rail Under Cover of SMGs Consignment Notes. https://treaties.un.org/doc/source/RecentTexts/XI_C_6_english.pdf, UN. 1952. International Convention to Facilitate the Crossing of Frontiers for Goods Carried by Rail. https://unece.org/DAM/trans/conventn/goodsraile.pdf.

3. Key Findings and Policy Recommendations: Toward Sustainable and Resilient Trade and Transport Facilitation

3.1 Key Findings

As detailed in Chapter 1, we understand that the Trade Cost Index produced by the WTO comprises five policy-relevant components: transport and travel costs, information and transaction costs, ICT connectedness, trade policy and regulatory differences, and governance quality. It also includes "others" for the aggregate of such costs not explained directly by the five determinants. Further in Chapter 2, we have studied the existing documents on trade and transport to identify its constituents across a comprehensive list of 6 clusters and 97 provisions along with the analysis of key transport agreements and conventions.

To evaluate the significance of the relative coverage of clusters, themes and provisions across the literature on trade and transport facilitation (as analyzed in Chapter 2) are mapped against the trade cost composition. The objective is to analyze key findings in the literature under review and subsequently identify the gaps for addressing high-impact areas for trade and transport facilitation. The mapping (Table 13) shows that clusters and themes impacting the bulk of trade costs are covered in relatively less width and depth across existing trade and transport facilitation frameworks and guidance documents. These themes include Stakeholder Involvement, Cross-Border Facilities, Transport, Trade Finance, SME Trade Facilitation, and Sustainable Trade Facilitation.

Figure 10 summarizes the findings in terms of identified gaps for coverage of provisions related to trade and transport facilitation themes across the literature reviewed in this study.

Table 13: Mapping Determinants of Trade Cost with Overall Coverage of Trade and Transport Facilitation Themes across Existing Guidance Documents

Trade Cost Composition for Goods (WTO) / Key TTF Thematic Clusters	Customs Procedures and Formalities		SPS/TBT	Stakeholder Coordination		Transit and Cross-Border Facilities		Transport	Trade Finance	Sustainability and Resilience	
	Simplification and Harmonization	Digitization	Standardization	Institutional Coordination/Capacity Building	Stakeholder Involvement	Transit	Cross-Border Facilities	Transport Infrastructure	Trade Finance	SME Trade Facilitation	Sustainable Trade
Transportation and Travel — 29%						High	Medium	(orange)			(orange)
Information and Transaction — 16%	High	High		High	Medium						
ICT Connectedness — 4%	High	High		High						(orange)	(orange)
Trade Policy and Regulatory Differences — 16%	High			High		High					
Governance Quality — 9%				High	Medium						
Others — 26%									Medium	(orange)	(orange)

High coverage , Medium coverage , Low coverage .

ICT = information and communication technology, SME= small and medium-sized enterprise, SPS/TBT = sanitary and phytosanitary/technical barriers to trade, TTF = transport and trade facilitation, WTO = World Trade Organization.

Source: WTO Cost Index and Its Determinants and study team's estimates.

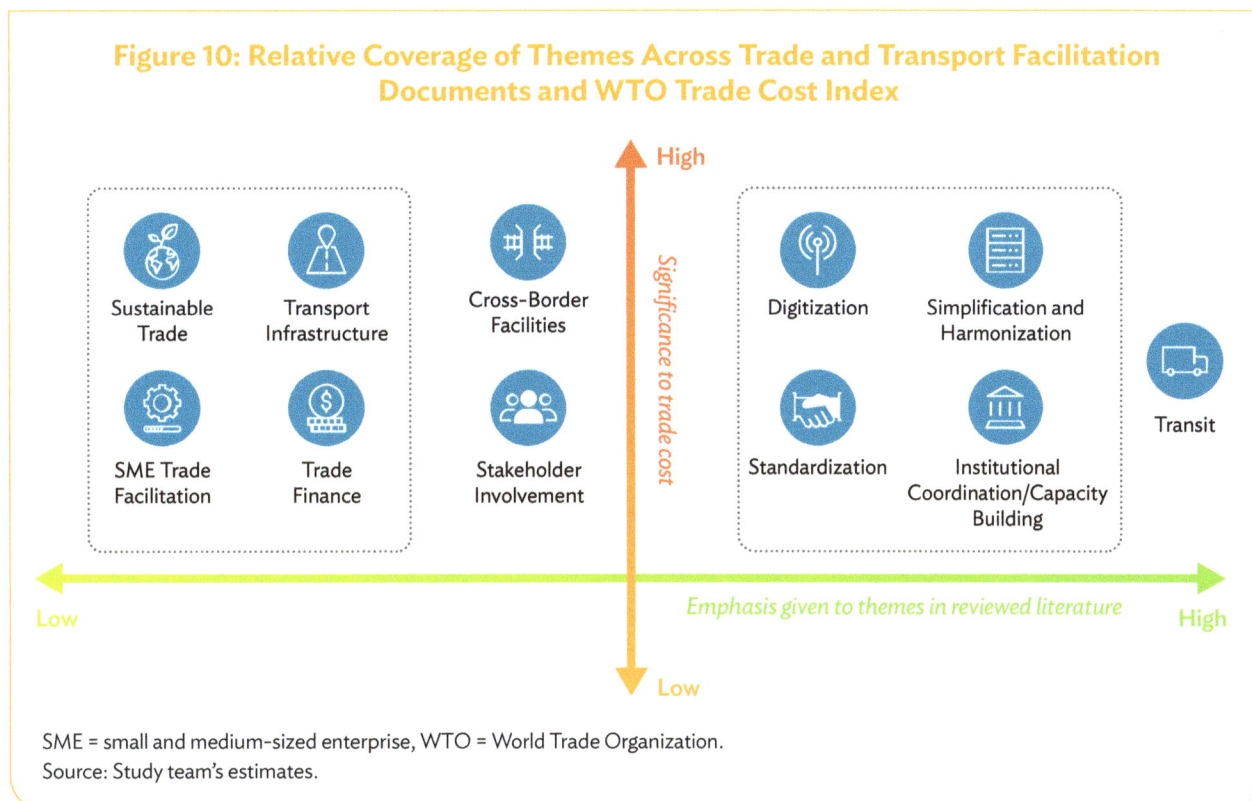

Figure 10: Relative Coverage of Themes Across Trade and Transport Facilitation Documents and WTO Trade Cost Index

SME = small and medium-sized enterprise, WTO = World Trade Organization.
Source: Study team's estimates.

3.2   Policy Recommendations

Based on the above findings, the study provides the following policy recommendations to enable sustainable trade and transport facilitation:

Provisions for sustainability and resilience need to be included.

"Others" costs in the Trade Cost Index constitute about 26% of overall trade cost. The mapping exercise put the Sustainability and Resilience cluster under the "others" determinant category of trade cost for two reasons: (i) the cluster is not directly represented by any of the five key cost determinants, and (ii) Sustainability and Resilience comprises important themes such as Sustainable Trade, SME Trade Facilitation, and Trade Finance. As discussed in Chapter 2, Sustainable Trade comprises disaster and crisis management, climate change mitigation, and gender sensitivity, which form a large group of important factors that impact the trade cost. Among the six clusters, this cluster is least covered in the trade and transport facilitation literature reviewed in this study.

Disaster management protocols: It is estimated that a large disaster can erode about 2% of a country's services exports and damage physical infrastructure and can close ports and restrict merchandise maritime shipping (Xu 2019). Chapter 2 already detailed how the COVID-19 pandemic caused many unforeseen disruptions in global trade and supply chain. Other disasters in 2020 accounted for $210 billion worth of economic losses (Insurance Information Institute n.d.).

During the COVID-19 pandemic, evidence suggests that most countries switched to adoption of ad hoc measures to mitigate impacts on trade. For example, Chile issued special resolutions to simplify and ensure business continuity at ports, airports, and border-crossing points (BCPs) (e.g., physical inspection without brokers presence and suspending paper documents). Cameroon relaxed controls for humanitarian aid consignments allowing immediate collection, pre-arrival completion of customs formalities, immediate removal of goods post inspection on the quayside/runway, and pre-arrival declaration procedures.

Adoption of ad hoc measures to mitigate the disruptions posed by the pandemic highlighted the need for integration of disaster management framework and crisis mitigation plans to tackle the negative impacts as emergency measures kicked in.

Within the literature on trade and transport facilitation reviewed in Chapter 2, the UN Global Survey on Digital and Sustainable Trade Facilitation is the only document with focus on emergency-related trade facilitation measures. The WTO has recommended a three-phase crisis response and resilience framework which can be incorporated in trade and transport facilitation frameworks (Table 14).

Table 14: Three-Phase Crisis Response and Recovery Framework

	Phase-1: Immediate Response	Phase 2: Recovery	Phase 3: Resilience
Trade-Related Measures: Goods	➡ Facilitate customs processes and procedures ➡ Ensure the quality and safety of relief items ➡ Temporary suspension of regular customs charges on the entry of relief items ➡ Access to goods of primary necessity: food supplies	➡ Financial support to enterprises to recover from damages ➡ Modification of tariff protection policies ➡ Resumption of exports ➡ Ensure the quality and safety of products exported by the disaster-affected country	➡ Define in advance domestic customs disciplines to be implemented in the event of a disaster ➡ Integrate disaster risk reduction measures into construction and restoration of buildings and physical infrastructures ("Build Smarter" approach) ➡ Increase resilience of the agriculture sector
Trade-Related Measures: Services	➡ Entry of foreign relief service providers ➡ Allocation of frequencies necessary for use of information and telecommunication (ITC) equipment ➡ Access to cash aid resources	➡ Financial support to local service suppliers ➡ Supply of services needed for reconstruction ➡ Procurement of goods and services needed for recovery ➡ Procurement for the purpose of providing international assistance	➡ Ensure automatic recognition of professional qualification of foreign relief service providers ➡ Encourage the supply of services needed in the event of disasters such as telecommunication services, insurance services, and environmental services (e.g., collection, processing, and disposal of waste) ➡ Improve the supply of weather-related services

Source: World Trade Organization. 2021. Trade Resilience in the Face of a Rising Burden of Natural Disasters. *Trade and Climate Change Information Brief No. 3*. Geneva.

Climate change mitigation: Greenhouse gas emissions generated by the production and transport of exported and imported goods and services have increased for decades and represent, on average, 20%–30% of global greenhouse gas emissions (WTO 2021). With trade and transport contributing a large share to greenhouse gas and CO_2 emissions, the principle causes for global warming and climate change, it is crucial to include climate change mitigation within the scope of trade facilitation. Existing guiding documents do not focus on the climate change aspects of trade facilitation.

While existing provisions pertaining to digitization and automation will contribute to some extent in reducing the carbon footprint of trade, the WTO provides more guidance to built-in provisions for climate change mitigation (WTO 2021b). They include:

(i)   Promoting new and efficient transport technologies, e.g., using sustainable and alternative fuels, and incentivizing substitution to more carbon-efficient alternative means of transportation (such as rail instead of road).

(ii) Members of the International Maritime Organization committed to reduce emissions by at least 50% by 2050 on 2008 levels, while pursuing complete decarbonization as soon as possible in this century.

(iii) Members of the International Civil Aviation Organization agreed to improve fuel efficiency by 2% annually through 2050 and to reach carbon neutral growth from 2020 onward.

(iv) The International Air Transport Association recently also agreed a plan to reach net zero carbon emissions by 2050 through use of sustainable aviation fuels, new aircraft technology, more efficient operations and infrastructure, and new zero-emissions energy source, such as hydrogen power.

(v)   Specific technical assistance to bridge capacity-building gaps in addressing the sustainability and resilience imperative through involvement of government, public and private sectors and development partners.

Small and medium-sized enterprises: SMEs represent about 90% of businesses and more than 50% of employment worldwide (International Trade Centre 2021), yet SMEs are responsible for an average of 33% of exports in selected developed countries, and only 18% of exports in selected developing countries (González and Sorescu 2019). SMEs still face disproportionate barriers to trade due to inadequate access to digital infrastructure, insufficient IT skills, and lack of financial resources. This was particularly the case in the context of COVID-19 (WTO 2020). Economic shocks, the introduction of new and unexpected customs requirements, increased costs, and constantly changing regulations from a whole raft of government agencies have compounded the difficulties faced by SMEs (UNESCAP 2021). SME-specific measures are covered only by surveys conducted by ADB-ESCAP and the UN Trade Facilitation (UNTF) survey within the literature reviewed in this study, and not specifically in trade facilitation frameworks.

Improvements in the trade facilitation environment would help firms of all sizes, but particularly benefit SMEs by reducing fixed and variable trade costs and integrating them into the global supply chains (OECD 2020). Specific provisions targeted at inclusion of SMEs which can form part of trade and transport facilitation frameworks include ensuring meaningful representation in NTFCs, inclusion in the Authorized Economic Operators scheme, access to single window portals, etc. Table 15 lists examples of economies which have implemented some of these provisions.

Table 15: Examples of Implementation of SME Trade Facilitation Measures

Economy	Digitization Adopted during the COVID-19 Pandemic
Australia; Hong Kong, China	Small and medium-sized enterprises (SMEs) have access to the Authorized Economic Operator (AEO) scheme. Australia distinguishes SMEs and provides a separate risk profile for them. Hong Kong, China provides additional incentives to AEO-certified firms to promote AEO certification for SMEs.
Paraguay	The EXPORTFACIL (easy export) system simplifies export for SMEs. SMEs must register in the Export Single Window. The benefits include reduced shipping rates, simplified export procedures, technical support, and among others.

Source: UN. 2021. Digital and Sustainable Trade Facilitation: Global Report 2021. https://www.unescap.org/kp/2022/untf-survey-2021-global.

Gender balance: Gender inequalities exist in various segments of the trade value chain, creating distinct barriers to women and preventing integration into international trade. The United Nation's Sustainable Development Goal 5 is to reduce gender inequalities and empower all women and girls. Empowering women to engage in trade will lead to stronger growth and a more prosperous society.

Women cross-border traders face significant challenges, including time constraints, costs of burdensome procedures, discrimination, and harassment at borders (UNCTAD 2022b). According to the World Customs Organization (WCO), only 37% of customs officials are women, however, at border posts almost all staff are men in positions of authority. Border posts can lack basic infrastructure such as stable telecommunications networks, separate sanitation facilities, etc., compounding gender-based barriers to trade, deterring trade facilitation. Provisions to mitigate gender inequalities are inadequately focused on in trade and transport facilitation frameworks, and are addressed only by the UN TF survey, among the guiding documents. Inclusion of gender in trade and transport facilitation frameworks is thus essential, with a wide range of solutions to reduce inequalities for women in trade.

Reducing gender inequality in trade facilitation is a difficult task, however, because inequalities are not strictly or explicitly declared in trade procedures (UN/CEFACT 2018). Provisions pertaining to domains such as transparency and accessibility will benefit trade stakeholders from all social groups, particularly reducing avenues for gender-based discrimination. UNCTAD has outlined a few specific provisions which can help (UNCTAD 2022). They include:

- Building a gender-sensitive NTFC or similar body: NTFCs should become gender-sensitive institutions with gender-balanced membership by establishing minimum representation of women in meetings and monitoring women traders' participation in activities.

- ➔ Incorporating outreach measures to target women stakeholders: Understanding trade facilitation reforms may be limited across stakeholders and women traders can be marginalized without fully benefiting from those initiatives. National authorities may find ways to translate trade regulations and legislation into indigenous languages and make them available for all.
- ➔ Addressing legal barriers to trade for women entrepreneurs and repealing gender-based discriminatory laws identified by NTFCs and women's business associations
- ➔ Setting up reporting mechanisms on gender-based discrimination: National authorities should establish individual complaint mechanisms for victims of gender-based discrimination at borders.
- ➔ Adopting client service charters for border agencies: Border agencies, preferably in collaboration with NTFCs, can adopt a client service charter with a code of conduct for public agents, stating the responsibilities and obligations of administrations towards women traders.
- ➔ Making inclusive and safe environments at borders: Border agency authorities should take steps to increase the proportion of women officials within their ranks. Also, infrastructure deficits near borders impact men and women differently and can create additional gander-based barriers to trade. Examples include lack of reliable access to electricity for lighting border crossings at night, limited access to a stable telecommunications network, absence of separate sanitation facilities for men and women, and lack of decent overnight accommodation.

Table 16 lists examples implemented by some of these provisions.

Table 16: Examples of Implementation of Gender Inequality Provisions

Country	Digitization Adopted during COVID-19
India	The National Trade Facilitation Action Plan 2020–2023 promotes gender inclusiveness. The plan has conceptualized the "Women in Global Business Program," which provides information, resources, and mentoring to Indian businesswomen.
Australia	The South Asia Regional Trade Facilitation Program, supported with Australian investment, promotes gender-sensitive trade facilitation. The program promotes women's participation in trade and transport and supports female traders at select land ports through public information campaigns.

Source: United Nations. 2021. Digital and Sustainable Trade Facilitation: Global Report 2021. https://www.unescap.org/kp/2022/untf-survey-2021-global.

Trade Finance: Access to trade finance is key to developing and including firms in regional and global supply chains. Trade finance indirectly facilitates increasing global trade and trade cash flows. The global trade finance gap was estimated at $1.7 trillion in 2020, up 15% from $1.5 trillion in 2018 (ADB 2021). COVID-19 has also exposed the vulnerability of paper-based trade financing, which requires significant in-person "back office" staffing. Provisions to ease trade finance could include easing of terms, working capital and liquidity support, bank-charge waivers, tax relief, access to trade finance from single windows, etc.

Table 17 lists provisions that can be covered in the Sustainability and Resilience cluster, as discussed in the section.

Table 17: Provisions in Sustainability and Resilience Cluster

Sr. No.	Sustainability and Resilience		
	Trade Finance	**SME Trade Facilitation**	**Sustainable Trade**
1	Enabling micro, small, and medium-sized enterprises' and women's access to finance	Allowing SMEs easier access to trade facilitation information and measures, improving digital capacities of SMEs, and providing training assistance for SMEs	Development of a three-phase crisis response and resilience framework for: (i) immediate response, (ii) recovery, and (iii) resilience
2	Provision of various export credit insurance tools with reduced administrative fees	Provision of access to single window portal to facilitate and enhance SME trade	Incentivizing new and efficient transport technologies, e.g., using sustainable and alternative fuels, and substitution to more carbon-efficient alternative means of transportation
3	Introduction of online trade finance facilities and provision of digital solutions for trade finance.	Inclusion of SME associations in National Trade Facilitation Committee (NTFC)	Specific technical assistance to bridge capacity-building gaps in addressing the sustainability and resilience imperative
4	Provision of single window mechanism to facilitate traders' access to finance	Inclusion of SMEs in Authorized Economic Operators scheme	Building a gender-sensitive NTFC or similar body
5	Reform banking practices and exchange controls to improve trade		Incorporation of outreach measures to target women stakeholders
6			Addressing legal barriers to trade for women entrepreneurs
7			Making at-the-border environment inclusive and safe, setting up reporting mechanism on gender-based discrimination, and adoption of client service charter for border agencies

SME = small and medium-sized enterprise.
Source: Trade and transport facilitation frameworks and guiding documents reviewed in Section 2.1, and study team's estimate.

Stronger provisions for clusters on transport and transit and cross-border facilities are needed.

Transportation and travel related costs constitute about 29% of overall trade costs. Provisions pertaining to this determinant lie within Transit and Cross-Border Facilities, and Transport. Chapter 2 sufficiently discussed the significance of transport enablement for trade facilitation. The trade and transport facilitation literature reviewed in this study does contain enabling guidance to cover essential aspects of transportation- and travel-related costs.

However, as Chapter 2 discussed, the WTO TFA and ASEAN Trade Facilitation Framework 2020 specifically does not contain enabling provisions for transport facilitation or physical connectivity and cross-border facilities. Regional trade facilitation frameworks, such as the ADB SASEC Operational Plan (2016–2025) and ADB CAREC Transport and Trade Facilitation Strategy, along with the World Bank Trade and Transport Facilitation Assessment, do contain enabling provisions. This study derives relevant provisions by combining guidance with that from reports such as the WCO's *Coordinated Border Management—An inclusive Approach for Connecting Stakeholders* and the ADB-ESCAP joint study on *Regional Cooperation for Trade and Transport Connectivity in the Age of Pandemics in Asia and the Pacific.*

Cross-Border Facilities

(i)   Physical infrastructure should be organized to facilitate smooth movement of goods-carrying vehicles and potential sources of bottlenecks should be identified and addressed.

(ii) Cross-border regulatory agencies should be equipped with the equipment and facilities to execute control and seek positive synergies by sharing such resources with each other.

(iii) Border infrastructure improvements to increase physical throughput capacity, possibly including modern equipment, ICT hardware and software, storage capacity, and passenger facilities.

Transport

(i)   Transport systems need to be developed with consideration for cross-border connectivity in compatibility, uniformity of standards, and infrastructure.

(ii)   Improvements in road transport need to focus on upgrading road conditions along major trade routes, enhancing the links to these routes, opening new trade routes, and enhancing accessibility to land and maritime borders.

(iii) Missing transport connectivity links need to be developed to increase geographic coverage and interconnectivity between corridors.

(iv)   Rail connectivity between ports and their hinterlands need to be enhanced to move trainload-type traffic to and from regionally connected seaports, especially for the transit of containers on high-volume routes. It will reduce the overall cost at the modal interface in the port, lower inland transit costs, and facilitate clearance with lower inventories.

(v)   Port infrastructure should be strengthened to enable the efficient handling of the subregion's maritime trade and expand capacity to cope with the anticipated growth in container traffic.

(vi)   Intermodal hubs should be developed to support efficient transfer of cargo between transport modes, specifically between rail and ocean carriers at gateway ports and between rail and road at intermodal rail yards.

(vii) Smart and sustainable transport connectivity solutions such as integrated transport management systems, intelligent transport systems, and digital logistic platforms, should be implemented to facilitate seamless and contactless transport, e.g., sustainable smart ports (ports operating with environmental impacts in mind). These ports utilize alternate energy sources for ships, reduce carbon footprints, implement solutions for decarbonization, etc.

Table 18 covers the provisions under the two clusters: Transit and Cross-Border Facilities and Transport Infrastructure.

Table 18: Provisions in Transit and Cross-Border Facilities and Transport Infrastructure

Sr. No.	Transit and Cross-Border Facilities		Transport Infrastructure
	Transit	Cross-Border Facilities	Transport
1	Through transport arrangements based on legal agreements	More efficient cargo handling and logistics services at the ports	Develop multimodal transport corridors to support market and value chain integration
2	Simplified and streamlined procedures at border crossings	Integrated check posts at border-crossing, improved physical infrastructure	Develop multimodal logistics hubs and improved telecommunications support
3	Designated priority lanes and green corridors for essential goods and designated truck stop and rest-area locations	Provision of warehouses	Streamline policies affecting organization of transport sector
4	Use of Transports Internationaux Routiers (TIR) (international road transports)/e-TIR system to facilitate transport and transit	Provision of cold storage	Adoption of modern management practices and technologies to improve scope and scale of transport sector
5	Pre-arrival processing of documentation	Provision of testing laboratories	Develop urban and line-haul transport interfaces
6	Clearance of relief consignments for export, transit, temporary admission, and import as a matter of urgency	Provision for designated truck-stop and rest-area locations	Developing policies on road safety and regular maintenance
7	Develop bilateral and multilateral transport agreements for seamless movement of goods	Automate border checks and processes	Promoting smart transport infrastructure, e.g., sustainable smart ports

Source: Trade and transport facilitation frameworks and guiding documents reviewed in Section 2.1, and project study team analysis.

Expedite implementation of key trade facilitation agreements and make them more efficient.

As Chapter 2 notes, most literature reviewed here, particularly the WTO TFA, addresses at-the-border issues of trade facilitation related to the clusters Customs Procedures and Formalities containing the themes Simplification and Harmonization, and Digitization, SPS/TBT with the Standardization theme, and Stakeholder Coordination containing the themes Institutional Coordination/Capacity Building and Stakeholder Involvement. These themes tackle the soft trade challenges related to institutional policies; trade procedures and practices; and technical barriers such as certification, institutional coordination, (domestic and international), etc.

During the pandemic, trade authorities were forced to make criteria and procedures restrictive to detect virus-infected commodities. Border processes grew more complex and time-consuming in most nations, and numerous commodities were delayed, giving precedence to COVID-19-related critical goods. While a lot of unforeseen firsts were witnessed in trade facilitation, such as circumstances related to quarantining of commodities and personnel, a comprehensive framework like the WTO TFA had a lot of provisions to cater to pandemic challenges.

The case for a WTO trade facilitation agreement

Even when armed with detailed knowledge and guidance for trade facilitation under the WTO, evidence suggests that countries had to undertake ad hoc measures to respond to the trade disruptions of the COVID-19 pandemic. The agreement already included procedures for expediting commodity movement, release, and clearance, including products in transit, among others. It also specifies procedures for efficient collaboration between customs and other border agencies, as well as competent authorities, on issues of trade facilitation and customs compliance. Table 19 captures examples of the strength of the WTO TFA's provisions in responding to disruptions like the COVID-19 pandemic.

Table 19: The Utility of the WTO TFA in Responding to COVID-19

Objective and Relevant Article within TFA	Use Cases in Wake of Responses to COVID-19 Pandemic
Expediting Import Procedures	
Pre-arrival processing: Pre-assess, identify, and prioritize import procedures in line with Articles 7.1. and 8.1(b) of the World Trade Organization (WTO) Trade Facilitation Agreement (TFA).	**Cameroon** allowed (i) pre-arrival completion of customs formalities, with inspection on quayside/runway and quick removal of the goods; and (ii) pre-arrival declaration procedures. Cameroon has a TFA implementation commitment of 68%.
Release upon arrival: Release goods prior to the submission of the goods declaration - Article 7.8.2(b)	**Brazil** allows the early release of goods, before an inspection and customs clearance, following the **World Customs Organization's HS classification reference documents**. Brazil has committed to a 100% TFA implementation.
Relaxing Procedures	
Minimizing requirements: Article 7.8.2(a) of the WTO TFA, documentation requirement can be minimized to seep up the release of expedited shipments.	The **European Union** (EU) waived the requirement to prove the empowerment for customs clearance activities carried out on behalf of the consignee. The EU has a 100% implementation of TFA.
Risk management: Bolster risk management and post-clearance audit - paragraphs 4 and 5 of Article 7 of the WTO TFA.	**Maldives:** Risk management to the maximum to expedite process and release consignments, and only the necessary items examined. Maldives has committed 16.4% implementation of TFA.
Promoting Transparency	
Transparency: WTO TFA contains 11 specific measures in Articles 1-5.	**Kenya** published information on COVID-19 trade-related emergency measures on **InfoTradeKenya Portal**. Kenya has committed a 7.6% implementation of TFA.

COVID-19 = coronavirus disease.

Source: United Nations Conference on Trade and Development. 2020. How Countries Can Leverage Trade Facilitation to Defeat the COVID-19 Pandemic. https://unctad.org/system/files/official-document/dtlinf2020d2_en.pdf, and the WTO TFA database https://www.wto.org/English/docs_e/legal_e/tfa-nov14_e.htm (accessed September 2022).

Case for UNESCAP's Framework Agreement on Facilitation of Cross-Border Paperless Trade in Asia and the Pacific

Digital trade facilitation was also critical in mitigating some pandemic disruptions and provided significant momentum for further trade digitization. The pandemic has motivated enhancement of digital infrastructure and expedited digital transformation in sectors where other paperless trade initiatives have lagged, such as electronic data and document sharing.

Implementation of UNESCAP's framework agreement on cross-border paperless trade would go a long way to reducing costs related to information and transactions, ICT connectedness and trade, and regulatory differences, which account for a combined tally of 36% in overall trade (Rubínová and Sebti 2021). A shared set of fundamental principles and a specialized intergovernmental platform for cross-border paperless commerce would help countries reduce trade costs and strengthen regional supply chains. Full implementation of paperless and cross-border paperless trade and TFA measures would help reduce overall global trade costs 13.5% (UN 2021). Box 2 showcases initiatives taken.

Box 2: Digitization and Paperless Trade Initiatives Implemented

→ Uzbekistan is implementing electronic sanitary and phytosanitary certificates based of existing global initiatives; India and the Eurasian Economic Union have accepted Electronic Certificates of Origin in response to the pandemic.

→ Australia is helping roll out the Automated System for Customs Data (ASYCUDA) World Trade Portal to help Pacific countries digitize trade processes.

→ Cameroon customs has deployed the country's new Customs Information System, replacing its customs automation system, ASYCUDA ++. The system automates procedures to increase paperless transactions and reduce human-to-human contact.

→ In Australia, paperless trade resulted in a savings of 1.5% for bulk sea shipments and 15% for air cargo.

Sources: ADB-ESCAP Regional Cooperation for Trade and Transport Connectivity in the Age of Pandemic, UN Digital and Sustainable Trade Facilitation: Global Report 2021.

Case for utilizing National Trade Facilitation Committees for strengthening stakeholder participation

Article 23.2 of the WTO TFA obliges countries to set up or maintain a coordination mechanism to support implementation of its trade facilitation provisions. While the TFA falls short of including provisions for transport and cross-border infrastructure for enabling trade (as discussed in Chapter 3), NTFCs have a broad-based composition which includes, among other things, public and private stakeholders pertaining to transport and cross-border infrastructure. Figure 11 shows composition of NTFCs from public and private entities.

Figure 11: Broad-Based Composition of National Trade Facilitation Committees

Public entities

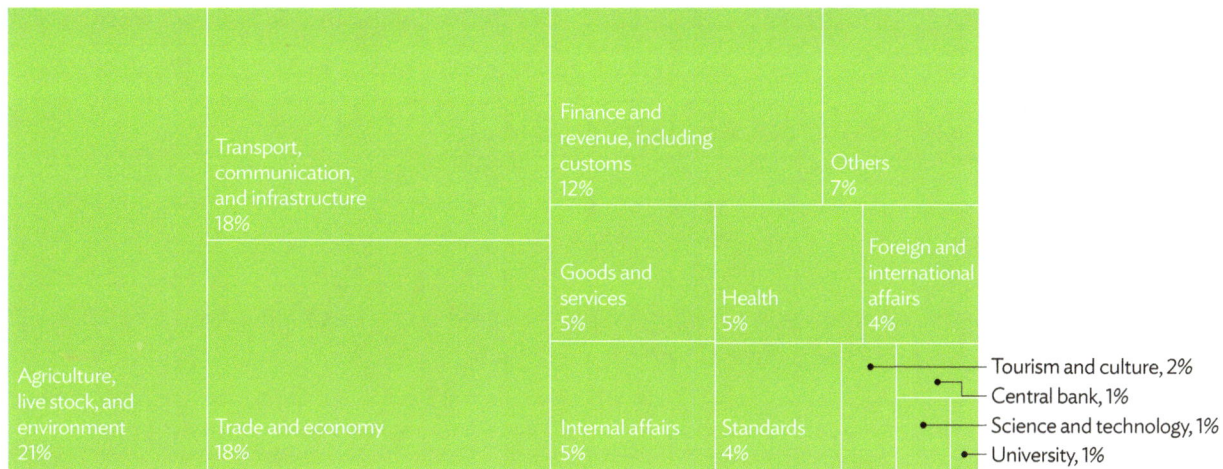

Agriculture, live stock, and environment 21%	Transport, communication, and infrastructure 18%	Finance and revenue, including customs 12%		Others 7%	
		Goods and services 5%	Health 5%	Foreign and international affairs 4%	
	Trade and economy 18%	Internal affairs 5%	Standards 4%		

Tourism and culture, 2%
Central bank, 1%
Science and technology, 1%
University, 1%

Private entities

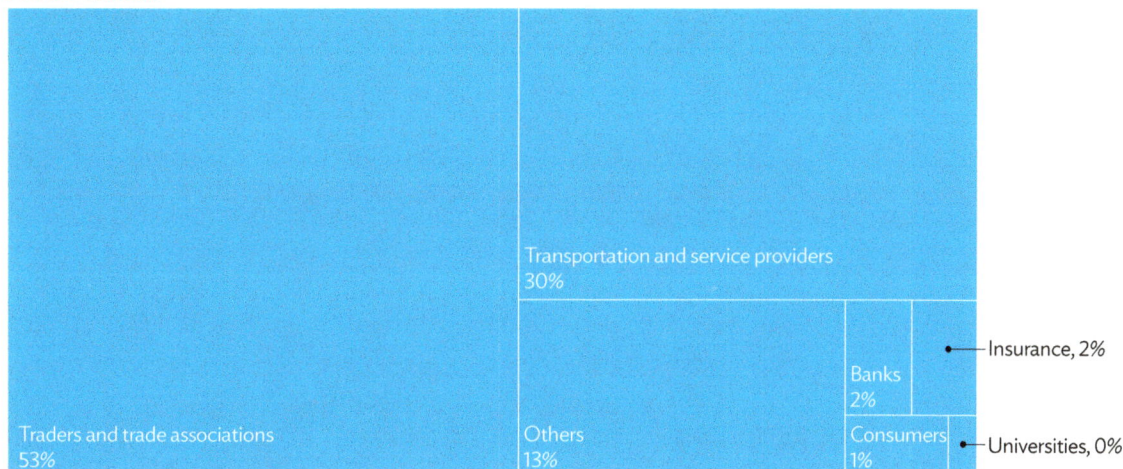

Traders and trade associations 53%	Transportation and service providers 30%		
	Others 13%	Banks 2%	Consumers 1%

Insurance, 2%
Universities, 0%

Source: United Nations Conference on Trade and Development. 2020. National Trade Facilitation Committees as Coordinators of Trade Facilitation Reforms. https://unctad.org/system/files/official-document/dtltlb2020d1_en.pdf.

UNCTAD's study on *National Trade Facilitation Committees as Coordinators of Trade Facilitation Reforms* identifies key trends that show that NTFCs are emerging as leading coordination mechanisms for coherent and all-inclusive trade facilitation policy reforms:

(i)   The vast majority of NTFCs have been officially institutionalized. Most committees are institutionalized at the governmental level, for instance, by a decision of the cabinet of ministers or by presidential decree.

(ii)   While coordination of implementation of the WTO TFA remains a core NTFC competency, in many countries the NTFCs also frequently act as donor coordinator for trade facilitation initiatives.

(iii) NTFCs are increasingly becoming more broad-based in constitution as the average membership is 18, where 12 participants represent the public sector and six for the private sector. NTFCs have seen the members increase since 2015, which is particularly important because trade facilitation is complex and requires a multistakeholder engagement from public and private participants.

(iv) The work of the committee has contributed to the mainstreaming of trade facilitation into other national policies in more than half of the countries.

(v) Most of the NTFCs meet regularly. Least-developed countries seem to be having more difficulties to ensure the regularity of the meetings, since more than a third of their NTFCs do not meet regularly and more than half of NTFCs usually meet on a quarterly basis.

Despite these positive developments in NTFC growth, the same study has highlighted a few areas where countries need to take appropriate action:

(i) Specific monitoring and evaluation tools for NTFCs are increasingly important, but many NTFCs are not equipped for this task.

(ii) Only a third of members of NTFCs are female. They are also rarely led by a woman. Just around a third of NTFCs in developing and least-developed countries are chaired or co-chaired by a woman. Most committees have never taken a decision or action to mainstream gender in trade facilitation.

(iii) Budget and financial resources for NTFCs are still scarce. The role of domestic resources toward sustaining the NTFC is increasingly apparent, and this is evident in the number of committees that become defunct or inactive after donor support dries up.

Table 20 summarizes trade facilitation provisions covered in various literature reviewed in this study.

Table 20: Provisions in Customs Procedures and Formalities, SPS/TBT, and Stakeholder Coordination Clusters

Sr. No.	Customs Procedures and Formalities		SPS/TBT	Stakeholder Coordination	
	Simplification and Harmonization	Digitization	Standardization	Institutional Coordination/Capacity Building	Stakeholder Involvement
1	Enhance transparency and predictability of customs actions	Upgrade to automated customs management systems	Identify SPS-sensitive products commodities and corresponding measures	Establish and/or operationalize trade facilitation committees	Strengthen public-private sector cooperation, collaboration, and partnership in improving the process, institutional, and infrastructural foundations of trade facilitation within the region

continued on next page

Table 20 *continued*

Sr. No.	Customs Procedures and Formalities		SPS/TBT	Stakeholder Coordination	
	Simplification and Harmonization	Digitization	Standardization	Institutional Coordination/Capacity Building	Stakeholder Involvement
2	Standardization and simplification of the goods declaration and supporting documents	Develop National Single Window project	Strengthen national conformity assessment boards – mutual recognition agreements	Build capacities linked to operational changes	Engage the business sector by providing easier access to official information on implementation and obtaining timely feedback on policies or measures
3	Minimum necessary customs control to ensure compliance with regulations	Leveraging information technology and facilitate more streamlined customs procedures and electronic exchange of information between transport and control authorities	Recognition of testing reports and certificates by competent authorities, as well as third parties for expedited clearance	Upgrade levels of ICT capacities to increase the automation processes	Conduct stakeholders' consultation on new draft regulations
4	Coordinated interventions with other border agencies	Facilitate electronic submission and exchange of documents	Setting up testing and laboratory facilities to meet SPS of main trading partners	Coordination, cooperation of border, domestic and cross-border agencies	Increase private sector participation in the management of public infrastructure
5	Establish standards that provide supply chain security and facilitation at a global level	Electronic application and issuance of import and export permits, certificate of origin	Implement electronic application and issuance of SPS certificates	Alignment of formalities and procedures with neighboring countries at border crossings	
6	Enable integrated supply chain management for all modes of transport	Enable e-payment of customs duties and fees			
7	Adoption of new simplified customs codes that are harmonized with international standards	Implement electronic application for customs refunds			
8	Strengthen risk management systems at border-crossing points to expedite clearance	Implement Economic and Social Commission for Asia and the Pacific framework agreement on cross-border paperless trade			
9	Simplify trade rules and procedures, remove/reduce restrictive or unnecessary practices	Institute national-level committee on paperless trade and supporting legal environment and regulatory policies			

continued on next page

Table 20 *continued*

| Sr. No. | Customs Procedures and Formalities | | SPS/TBT | Stakeholder Coordination | |
	Simplification and Harmonization	Digitization	Standardization	Institutional Coordination/Capacity Building	Stakeholder Involvement
10	Nondiscriminatory rules and procedures				
11	Access to adequate legal appeal procedures				
12	Allowing trusted traders/authorized economic operators with expedited clearance				
13	Advance publication/ notification of new trade-related regulations before their implementation				
14	Establishment and publication of average release times				

ICT = information and communication technology, SPS/TBT = sanitary and phytosanitary/technical barriers to trade.
Source: Trade and transport facilitation frameworks and guiding documents reviewed in Section 2.1 and study team's estimates

Institutional arrangement for integrated approach

As per the WTO Trade Cost Index detailed in Chapter 1, the theme pertaining to Stakeholder Involvement impacts two key determinants of the trade cost: information and transaction (16%) and governance quality (9%). Facilitation of international trade and transport involves many government agencies and authorities as well as public and private entities nationally, regionally, and subnationally. Article 8 of the WTO TFA talks on the need for border agency cooperation withing countries and with the neighboring countries. The previous section described how NTFCs can strengthen stakeholder participation (Tables 21 and 22 provide a comprehensive composition of public and private stakeholders) in countries' trade and transport activities. The study team has identified around 27 key public and private stakeholders relevant for trade and transport facilitation that have a role and interest across the 6 clusters and 11 themes.[7]

---

[7] The reference for the stakeholders name is taken for India, the corresponding departments in other Asia and Pacific countries might have different connotations and additional agencies with a role across the 11 themes.

Table 21: List of Identified Public Stakeholders

Trade Facilitation Stakeholders Mapped across Enabling Themes in Terms of Their Relevance	Customs Procedures and Formalities	Standardization	Institutional Coordination/ Capacity Building	Digitization	Transit	Cross-Border Facilities	Trade Finance	Stakeholder Involvement	Transport Infrastructure	SME Trade Facilitation	Sustainable Trade
Customs Authority	■		■							■	
Trade Facilitation Comms/Trading Corporation	■		■							■	■
Department of Foreign Trade							■	■			
Logistics Division									■		
Ministry of Civil Aviation									■		
MSME Department			■				■	■		■	
Export Promotion Councils				■			■				
Banks							■				
Food Safety agency		■				■					
Quarantine/Plant Protection agencies/Department of Agri/Horti		■				■					
Wildlife Bureau/Animal Quarantine/Animal Husbandry		■									
Inspection Councils											
National Standard Bodies		■									
Pollution Control Board											■
Ministry of Electronics and IT			■	■							
Ministry of Home Affairs				■		■					
Ministry of Health		■									
Warehousing Corporation											

Public

ICT = information and communication technology; IT = information technology, MSME = micro, small, and medium-sized enterprise; SME = small, and medium-sized enterprise.

Source: United Nations. Trade Facilitation Implementation Guide. https://tfig.unece.org/contents/stakeholders.htm (accessed in 2022).

Table 22: List of Identified Private Stakeholders

Trade Facilitation Stakeholders Mapped across Enabling Themes in Terms of Their Relevance	Customs Procedures and Formalities	Standardization	Institutional Coordination/ Capacity Building	Digitization	Transit	Cross-Border Facilities	Trade Finance	Stakeholder Involvement	Transport Infrastructure	SME Trade Facilitation	Sustainable Trade
Chamber of Commerce				✓			✓	✓			✓
E-commerce Companies				✓			✓			✓	
Industry Associations		✓	✓					✓		✓	✓
Women Committees			✓								
Freight Forwarders			✓		✓				✓		
Customs House Agency						✓					
Testing and Certification Agencies		✓									
Port/Dry Port Operators					✓	✓			✓		
CFS Operators					✓	✓			✓		

Private

CFS = container freight station, SME = small, and medium-sized enterprise.

Source: United Nations. Trade Facilitation Implementation Guide. https://tfig.unece.org/contents/stakeholders.htm (accessed in 2022).

Internal border agency cooperation

Article 8.1 of the WTO TFA has emphasized the regional cooperation of border agencies for trade facilitation. Efficient and effective coordination among all identified government agencies and authorities, and good collaboration between the public and private sectors, are crucial for formulation and implementation of international trade facilitation measures. Creation of a coordinated trade environment helps businesses trade more easily with predictable procedures, streamlined regulations, efficient usage of human resources, and added stakeholder benefits. The NTFCs have been officially institutionalized as a solution in a number of countries to involve relevant stakeholders for an integrated approach to trade and transport facilitation (WTO 2022). However, as discussed in Section 3.2, the average membership of NTFCs across countries who have formalized the committee is only 18 (12 public sector and 6 private sector) instead of the complete representation of all stakeholders in a country. Box 3 looks at Thailand.

Box 3: National Committee on Trade Facilitation in Thailand

Thailand ratified the World Trade Organization Trade Facilitation Agreement (WTO TFA) in October 2015 and established the National Committee on Trade Facilitation (NCTF, inter-changeably used in place of NTFC by literatures as sourced below) in June 2017 and the working group under NCTF in January 2018.

The NCTF has a subcommittee chaired by the permanent secretary or deputy permanent secretary of the Ministry of Commerce, with directors general of relevant agencies as members. The NCTF consists of 19 agencies (15 public and 4 private). The key ministries and departments represented in NCTF are the Ministry of Commerce, Department of Trade Negotiations, Ministry of Finance, Department of Foreign Trade, Ministry of Foreign Affairs, Customs Department, Ministry of Agricultural and Cooperatives, Ministry of Industry, Ministry of Transport, Ministry of Public Health, etc., and the key private sector representatives are the Thai Chamber of Commerce, Thai National Shippers' Council, Federation of Thai Industries, and Thai Bankers' Association.

Although Thailand has a functional NTFC, private sector membership of the committee, including its working group, should be ensured. A regular consultation mechanism for micro, small, and medium-sized enterprises should be established/enhanced, leveraging existing groupings or associations.

Sources: World Trade Organization, Trade Facilitation Agreement Database. 2019. Experience Sharing: National Committee on Trade Facilitation. WTO TFA database. https://tfadatabase.org/trade-facilitation-committee/experience-sharing/topic/art-23-2-national-committee-on-trade-facilitation; S. Buban, P. Chammanakij, and J. Jangsawang. 2021. Towards Seamless Trade Facilitation in ASEAN: Results from the ASEAN Seamless Trade Facilitation Indicators Baseline Study. Economic Research Institute for ASEAN and East Asia. https://www.eria.org/uploads/media/Research-Project-Report/2021-08-Towards-Seamless-Trade-Facilitation-ASEAN/15_Ch.10-Thailand-Report.pdf.

Countries such as Canada—though it has representation of around 25 national, private sector associations representing diverse sectors, and senior Canada Border Services Agency executives—have kept preexisting intergovernmental avenues of communication and mechanisms for consulting with private sector stakeholders, including in Canada's case the Border Commercial Consultative Committee. These processes serve as the national coordinating committee in accordance with Article 23.2, so it is not a newly established committee. These preexisting networks enable Canada to coordinate trade facilitation domestically, liaise with industry, and implement the TFA(WCO 2015).

Cross-border agency cooperation

Article 8.2 of the WTO TFA stresses mutual cooperation on agreed terms of agency of member countries who share a common border to coordinate procedures at border crossings to facilitate cross-border trade, particularly for SMEs; reduce duplication of paperwork and the associated cost; and enhance safety to limit illicit/anti-terrorist activities. The OECD Trade Facilitation Indicator also uses the factors identified by WTO TFA along with other factors (as tabulated in Table 23) to measure and score the cross-border coordination scenario at the country level (OECD 2018).

Table 23: Factors Impacting Cross-Border Cooperation

WTO TFA Factors OECD Considers	Additional Factors OECD Considers
Alignment of working days and hours	Institutional and legal framework enabling coordination
Alignment of procedures and formalities	Exchange of data and harmonization of requested documentation
Development and sharing of common facilities	Mutually recognized authorized operator schemes
Joint controls	Well-established communication among agencies
Establishment of one-stop border post control	Mutually recognized processes and procedures, inspections, and controls

OECD = Organisation for Economic Co-operation and Development, WTO TFA = World Trade Organization Trade Facilitation Agreement.
Source: OECD. 2018. Trade Facilitation and the Global Economy. https://www.oecd-ilibrary.org/sites/9789264277571-5-en/index. html?itemId=/content/component/9789264277571-5-en.

Despite the benefits to trade facilitation and cost reduction, implementation of cross-border cooperation is a challenge across the globe due to reasons such as lack of existing procedures for sharing information across agencies internationally, and limited ICT capacity to develop new protocols for document management and simplification of procedures. A major factor hindering cross-border coordination is the prevalence of political and institutional limitations, such as border disputes (Brunet-Jailly 2022).

However, there are exceptions to these observations, such as the European Union (EU), where powerful positive and mediating power of the EU institutions and policies on border issues encourage cross-border coordination, cooperation, and collaboration, spanning internal and external boundaries of the member states. Other such examples are Hong Kong, China; and Singapore. Box 4 presents the case of Finland, Norway, and Sweden on establishing joint inspection to save time and cost.

> ## Box 4: Cross-Border Agency Coordination
>
> **Finland, Norway, and Sweden:** Cooperation between these three countries is built on the division of labor, in which national border authorities of each country are allowed to provide services and exercise the legal powers of their home country and the neighboring country. For instance, when goods are exported from Norway, all paperwork related to both exports and imports may be attended by either Swedish, Finnish, or Norwegian customs officers.
>
> Source: The Standing Committee for Economic and Commercial Cooperation. 2016. Improving the Border Agency Cooperation among the OIC Member States for Facilitating Trade. https://www.comcec.org/wp-content/uploads/2021/07/8-TRD-AR.pdf.

As per the 2016 report *Improving the Border Agency Cooperation among the OIC Member States for Facilitating Trade* by the Standing Committee for Economic and Commercial Cooperation, efforts are ongoing by border-control agencies for international cooperation on border management matters. However, several innovative activities have not yet been fully exploited, especially in less-developed parts of the world. For example, one-stop border posts are a promising solution for facilitating cross-border traffic between two neighboring countries. Investments in training and education are suitable for increasing general awareness of the benefits of border agency cooperation.

It is thus critical for trading nations to design and implement mechanisms for suitable policy and action plans to improve internal and cross-border agency cooperation to enhance trade and transport facilitation.

4. Measuring National and Subnational Trade Readiness

4.1 Objective

This study, so far, has identified six clusters covering 11 themes and 97 provisions of trade and transport facilitation. It has also summarized major frameworks and their metrics for evaluation of effectiveness of trade facilitation. This chapter takes a step forward to derive tangible outcomes from this exercise.

It ties the outputs of previous chapters together to suggest diagnostic frameworks for national and subnational trade readiness. These readiness assessments aim to enable users to conduct an evaluation across both hard and soft dimensions of trade and transport facilitation. National readiness is assessed at the country level, and subnational readiness is assessed at a trade point within a country or across countries, such as trade corridors. Trade points can be within a country or at national boundaries as well, for example, at border points in transnational corridors. The readiness is assessed on the basis of performance across trade and transport facilitation clusters identified in this study.

4.2 Diagnostic Framework for National-Level Trade Readiness

Structure of the framework

The national-level trade readiness will assess the relative position of a country across various clusters of trade and transport facilitation. To obtain a measurable, comparable, and easily replicable point of view of a country's strength across various trade and transport facilitation clusters, the study has used trade facilitation indicators from various trade indices, summarized in Table 24. These are published regularly globally for a large group of countries, as are additional indicators for clusters such as Transport and Sustainability and Resilience, which evaluate their respective themes and provisions, e.g., World Bank's Logistics Performance Index. Table 24 details relevant indicators from the indexes.[8]

---

[8] These 46 indicators have been obtained from the seven global indexes, such as the World Bank's Logistics Performance Index (LPI) or the OECD TFI, etc., for measuring national trade readiness. The indexes are a group of indicators based on relevant themes, e.g., logistics performance is the theme measured by the LPI, which is eventually measured by multiple indicators such as efficiency of customs and border management clearance, quality of logistics services, etc.

Table 24: Indicators for National Trade Readiness

Clusters	Key Indicators of Measurement	Indexes
Customs Procedures and Formalities ⮕ Simplification and Harmonization ⮕ Digitization	Efficiency of customs and border management clearance ("customs")	World Bank's Logistics Performance Index (WBG LPI)
	Trading across borders - transport and border compliance	World Bank's Ease of Doing Business
	Authorized operators program implementation	Organisation for Economic Co-operation and Development Trade Facilitation Indicator (OECD TFI)
	Conduct post-clearance audits	OECD TFI
	Established rules for appeal procedures	OECD TFI
	Transparent policy making - publication and consultation	OECD TFI
	Use of automated risk management	OECD TFI
	Accessibility to applicable legislation	OECD TFI
	Single window implementation	OECD TFI
	Implementation of electronic declaration systems	OECD TFI
	Number electronically processed procedures	OECD TFI
	Electronic payment processing system	OECD TFI
	General coordination between agencies	OECD TFI
	Adherence to international standards for customs	OECD TFI
	Advance publication of regulations	OECD TFI
	Procedures simplification	OECD TFI
	Accessibility of customs financing provisions	OECD TFI
	Use of digital certificates	OECD TFI
SPS TBT	Mutual recognition agreements	OECD TFI
Transit and Cross-Border Facilities	24/7 automated processing of customs declaration	OECD TFI
	Established procedures for pre-arrival processing	OECD TFI
Stakeholder Coordination ⮕ Institutional Coordination/ Capacity Building ⮕ Stakeholder Involvement	Internal coordination between domestic agencies	OECD TFI
	Coordinated Infrastructure use	OECD TFI
	Institutionalized mechanism to support inter-agency coordination	OECD TFI
	Cross-border coordination with border agencies	OECD TFI
	Cross-border harmonization of the different computer systems	OECD TFI
	Cross-border staff training programs	OECD TFI
	Control delegation between agencies	OECD TFI
	Public consultations between traders and other interested parties and government	OECD TFI

continued on next page

Table 24 *continued*

Clusters	Key Indicators of Measurement	Indexes
	Number of targeted stakeholder groups	OECD TFI
	Policy objectives communication	OECD TFI
Transport Infrastructure	Competence and quality of logistics services—trucking, forwarding, and customs brokerage ("Quality of logistics services")	WBG LPI
	The quality of trade and transport infrastructure ("Infrastructure")	WBG LPI
	Availability and quality of domestic infrastructure across four modes - road, rail, air, and sea	World Economic Forum Global Enabling Trade Index Pillar 4: Infrastructure
	Frequency with which shipments reach consignees within scheduled or expected delivery times ("Timeliness")	WBG LPI
	Ease of arranging competitively priced shipments (ease of arranging shipments")	WBG LPI
	Ability to track and trace consignments ("Tracking and tracing")	WBG LPI
Sustainability and Resilience ➲ Trade Finance ➲ Sustainable Trade ➲ SME Trade Facilitation	Percentage of SMEs in authorized operators	OECD TFI
	Environmental pillar score	Hinrich's Sustainable Trade Index 2020
	Women workplace indicator	World Bank Open Data
	Women entrepreneurship and access to finance	
	Implementation of TF measures for women	United Nations Digital and Sustainable Trade Facilitation
	Implementation of TF measures for SMEs	
	Country signatory to Paris Agreement	United Nations Sustainable Development Goals website
	Country Commitment to net zero emissions by 2050	Net Zero tracker website
	Firms using banks to finance investment	World Bank open data

SME = small and medium-sized enterprise, SPS TBT= sanitary and phytosanitary technical barriers to trade, TF = trade facilitation.
Source: Reports published on respective indexes: details are provided in Appendix 3.

Approach for calculation

These indices vary across the time period to which data used in their analysis belongs. For example, as Table A.12 in Appendix 3 shows, latest values for the World Bank's Logistics Performance Index are available for 2018 and for OECD TFI for 2019. Also, these indices vary in their methodology for evaluating absolute and relative positions of countries under study. For example, the World Bank's Ease of Doing Business followed a survey-based approach and the data is captured in the form of a rank based on scoring between 0 to 100, where 100 indicates the best case. OECD TFI also follows a survey-based approach, but the data is captured as a score between 0, 1, and 2, with 2 the best case.[9]

[9] The World Bank Doing Business has been currently discontinued and is formulating a new approach to assessing the business and investment climate in economies worldwide.

To create a uniform scale of evaluation for all the metrics, the framework comprises calculation of percentiles for the country in focus for the reference sample (global or regional). This will give a relative position of a country in each evaluation metric.

4.3   Diagnostic Framework for Subnational Trade Readiness

Structure of the framework

Subnational readiness aims to assess a trade gateway across countries (border-crossing point at land, port, airport, etc.) in the following thematic areas:

- **At-the-border facilities/transit cross-border facilities:** The evaluation would be based on the availability and quality of the at-the-border infrastructure across roads, rails, etc.
- **Competence and quality of services:** The parameter aims to evaluate the competence and quality of services (cost and lead time) provided by each institution (roads, rails, ports, airports, warehousing, etc.) in cross-border transit.
- **Process efficiency:** The evaluation of processes in cross-border trade and transit depends on the time taken for export import clearances, the number of agencies involved in the processes, electronic submission of documents at the customs station, etc.
- **Sources of major delays:** The parameters look into areas and processes that cause unnecessary delays, such as compulsory transloading, informal payments, etc.

Forty-three key indicators across the six key clusters and the abovementioned themes have been identified for developing the subnational-level trade readiness assessment framework. These draw inspiration from studies such as World Bank's Domestic LPI structure of themes and evaluation metrics used in studies such as the report *Cambodia Trade Corridor Performance Assessment* and ADB's study *Breaking Barriers: Leveraging Mongolia's Transport and Logistics Sector* (World Bank 2014) (ADB 2018). Values for indicators for subnational assessment have to be compiled from secondary sources such as websites, data banks, annual reports, notifications of respective agencies, technical studies, etc. Where values for indicators are not available from secondary sources, primary research with relevant stakeholders will have to be conducted to fill those gaps.[10]

Table 25 details the subnational readiness assessment framework. The 43 identified indicators have been mapped with the six clusters and the four themes as discussed above.

Approach for calculation

For assessment, the indicators' performance of a region under focus are benchmarked against a contextual scenario. This would provide comparative information of the region on whether the performance is above or below average for each of the indicators.

---

[10]   A sample questionnaire is provided in Appendix 5 as a guide.

Table 25: Subnational Readiness Assessment Framework

Parameters	Indicator	Stakeholder Involved		Border Facilities	Competence and Quality	Process Efficiency	Sources of Major Delays
		Public Stakeholders	Private Stakeholders				
Customs Procedures and Formalities and Stakeholder Coordination							
Customs Clearance Process	Average time taken for import clearance	Customs authority	Traders, exporters, importers, trade associations, logistics service providers, transport associations			■	
	Percent of import declarations cleared electronically					■	
	Average time taken for export clearance	Customs authority	Traders, exporters, importers, trade associations			■	
	Percent of export declarations cleared electronically					■	
	Rate duplication of bureaucratic activities	Customs authority	Traders, exporters, importers, trade associations		■		
	Border clearance cost	Customs authority	Traders, exporters, importers, trade associations		■		
	Provision of digital payments					■	
Pre-Shipment Inspection	Time taken for pre-shipment physical inspection	Customs authority	Traders, exporters, importers, trade associations				■
	Percentage of physical Inspection						■
Solicitation of Informal Payments	Prevalence of informal payments for cargo clearance, checkpoints, weighbridge stations, etc.	Customs authority	Traders, exporters, importers, trade associations, transport associations				■
Cross-Border Coordination	Synchronization of border timings, clearance procedures					■	
	Presence of international agreements					■	
Transit Cross-Border Facilities and SPS TBT							
Warehousing, Transloading Facilities	Total no. of warehousing facilities	Warehousing associations, corporation	Transport associations, freight forwarders, logistics service providers	■			
	Presence of transshipment yard			■			
	Cost of warehousing and transloading				■		
	Compulsory warehousing, transloading process						■

continued on next page

Table 25 continued

Parameters	Indicator	Stakeholder Involved		Border Facilities	Competence and Quality	Process Efficiency	Sources of Major Delays
		Public Stakeholders	Private Stakeholders				
Telecommunications and IT	Presence of ICT infrastructure	Department of IT and Telecommunications	Traders, exporters, importers, trade associations	✓			
	Availability of internet and mobile connectivity						
Export Processing Zones	Presence of SEZs	Logistics division, customs authority	Industry associations, MSMEs	✓			
	Presence of custom bonded warehouses						
Quality, Standards Inspection Agencies	Presence of inspection facilities	Inspection agencies, councils	Traders, exporters, importers, trade associations			✓	
	Operation of risk management system			✓			
Health, SPS Agencies	Presence of quarantine facilities	SPS agencies	Traders, trade associations				
Other Facilities	Presence of x rays, scanners, weighbridges, etc.		All of the above				
Transport Infrastructure and Sustainability and Resilience							✓
Maritime Transport	Fees charged by port	Ministry/ Department of Ports/Regional Port Authority/Ministry of Commerce	Traders, exporters, importers, trade associations		✓		
	Annual capacity				✓		
	Total no. of available terminals				✓		
	Total no. of available berths				✓		
	Utilization percentage						
	Size of containers handled			✓	✓		
Air Transport	Airport charges for cargo transit	Airports authorities/ Civil aviation	Traders, exporters, importers, trade associations				
	Time taken for cargo processing					✓	
Road	Connectivity of a BCP to a national highway/carriageway/expressway	National Highway Authority, Logistics Division, Road and Transport Authority, Ministry of Commerce	Transport associations, freight forwarders, logistics service provider	✓			
	Type of laning of the connecting road				✓		
	Availability of parking area			✓			
	No. of cargo trucks, capacity of trucks exchanged per day				✓		

continued on next page

Table 25 *continued*

Parameters	Indicator	Stakeholder Involved		Border Facilities	Competence and Quality	Process Efficiency	Sources of Major Delays
		Public Stakeholders	Private Stakeholders				
	Rates of road transport				●		
	Average time taken for cross-border cargo transport					●	
Rail	Presence of operational rail line and haul infrastructure	Railway Authority, Ministry of Commerce	Transport associations, freight forwarders, logistics service providers	●			
	Type of rail gauge in use				●		
	Rail transport rates				●		
Freight Forwarders, Logistics Service Providers, Shippers	Charges by freight forwarders	Ministry of Environment, Ministry of Transport	Transport associations, freight Forwarders, logistics service providers			●	
	Type of trucks used						

BCP = border-crossing point; ICT = information and communication technology; MSME = micro, small, and medium-sized enterprise, SEZ = special economic zone, SPS TBT = sanitary and phytosanitary technical barriers to trade.

Source: World Bank. Logistics Performance Index. https://lpi.worldbank.org/; World Bank. 2014. Cambodia Trade Corridor Performance Assessment. Washington, DC. https://openknowledge.worldbank.org/handle/10986/20763; Asian Development Bank. 2018. Leveraging Mongolia's Transport and Logistics Sector. Manila and study team's estimates.

4.4 Illustrative Case Study for National and Subnational Trade Readiness Assessment

Overview of the case study subject

The GMS Program is the result of a 1992 economic cooperation and integration agreement among Cambodia, the Lao PDR, Myanmar, Thailand, Viet Nam, and Yunnan Province of the People's Republic of China (PRC). The GMS is an integral part of the movement toward a greater Asian economic community (ADB 2016). The section of the Southern Economic Corridor spanning Thailand and Cambodia—Aranyaprathet and Poipet—has been selected as a case study subject. Accordingly, national assessment has been done for Thailand and Cambodia and subnational assessment for the Aranyaprathet and Poipet border points (Figure 12).

Figure 12: Southern Economic Corridor Spanning Thailand and Cambodia

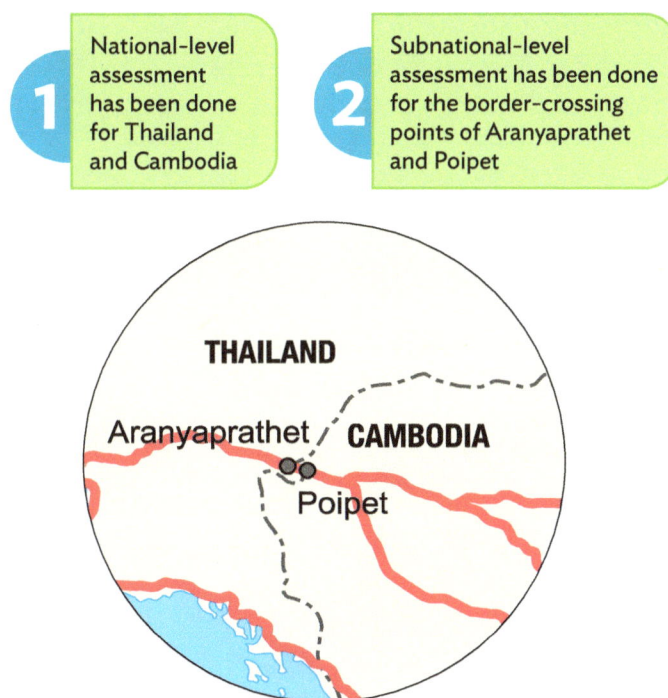

Source: Asian Development Bank. 2018. Review of Configuration of The Greater Mekong Subregion Economic Corridors. Manila. https://www.adb.org/sites/default/files/institutional-document/400626/gms-corridors-configuration-review.pdf.

Measuring National Readiness

Based on the national readiness framework developed in the previous section, a sample readiness assessment has been conducted for the economies of Cambodia and Thailand on 46 indicators across the six identified clusters as per the national-level trade readiness framework developed in Section 4.2. Figures 13 and 14 present the scatter plots of the calculated percentile for Thailand and Cambodia across global, Asian, and Southeast Asian samples.

Key inferences from the figures above are as follows:

- Thailand is better placed across all indicators of Transport Infrastructure, with percentiles around 50% and above those of global, Asian, and Southeast Asian samples.
- For the Customs Procedures and Formalities cluster, about half of indicators score a percentile of 50% and above for Thailand.
- For SPS TBT, Transit and Cross-Border Facilities, and Stakeholder Coordination, Thailand has a comparatively lower percentile (below 50%) for the majority of the indicators across global, Asian, and Southeast Asian samples.
- Cambodia's percentile for the majority of the indicators across the six clusters is below 50%, relative to global, Asian and Southeast Asian samples.
- All countries in Southeast Asia are signatories to the Paris Agreement, hence, the percentile of Thailand for the indicator in the Southeast Asian sample is 0%.
- All countries in Southeast Asia have commitments to net zero by 2050, hence, the percentile of Thailand for the indicator in the Southeast Asian sample is 0%.

Figure 13: Position of Thailand
(%)

Clusters

Cluster	Indicator
Sustainability and Resilience	Country commitment to net zero emissions by 2050
	Country signatory to Paris Agreement
	WBG indicator: Firms using banks to finance investment
	WBG indicator: Women entrepreneurship and access to finance
	WBG indicator: Women workplace indicator
	UN: Implementation of TF measures for women
	UN: Implementation of TF measures for SMEs
	Hinrich foundation: Environmental pillar score
	OECD: Percentage of SMEs in authorized operators
Transport Infrastructure	WBG LPI: Tracking and tracing of consignments
	WBG LPI: Ease of arranging shipments
	WBG LPI: Delivery timeliness
	WBG LPI: Quality of trade and transport Infrastructure
	WBG LPI Indicator: Logistics competence
	WEF Pillar 4: Availability and quality of transport infrastructure
Stakeholder Coordination	OECD: Policy objectives communication
	OECD: Number of targeted stakeholder groups
	OECD: Public consultations between traders and other parties and government
	OECD: Control delegation between agencies
	OECD: Cross-border staff training programs
	OECD: Cross-border harmonization of the different computer systems
	OECD: Cross-border coordination
	OECD: Institutionalized mechanism to support inter-agency coordination
	OECD: Coordinated infrastructure use
	OECD: Internal coordination between domestic agencies
SPS TBT and Transit and Cross-Border Facilities	OECD: Established procedures for pre-arrival processing
	OECD: 24/7 automated processing of customs declaration
	OECD: Mutual recognition agreements (MRAs)
Customs Procedure and Formalities	OECD: Use of digital certificates
	OECD: Customs financing provisions
	OECD: Procedures simplification
	OECD: Advance publication of regulations
	OECD: Adherence to international standards
	OECD: General coordination between agencies
	OECD: Electronic payment processing system
	OECD: Number electronically processed procedures
	OECD: Implementation of electronic declaration systems
	OECD: Single window implementation
	OECD: Accessibility to applicable legislation
	OECD: Use of automated risk management
	OECD: Policy-making transparency-publication and consultation
	OECD: Established rules for appeal procedure
	OECD: Conduct post-clearance audits
	OECD: Authorized operators program implementation
	WBG EoDB: Trading across borders
	WBG LPI: Customs and border management

Percentiles: 0, 20, 40, 60, 80, 100

● Global   ● Asia   ● South East Asia

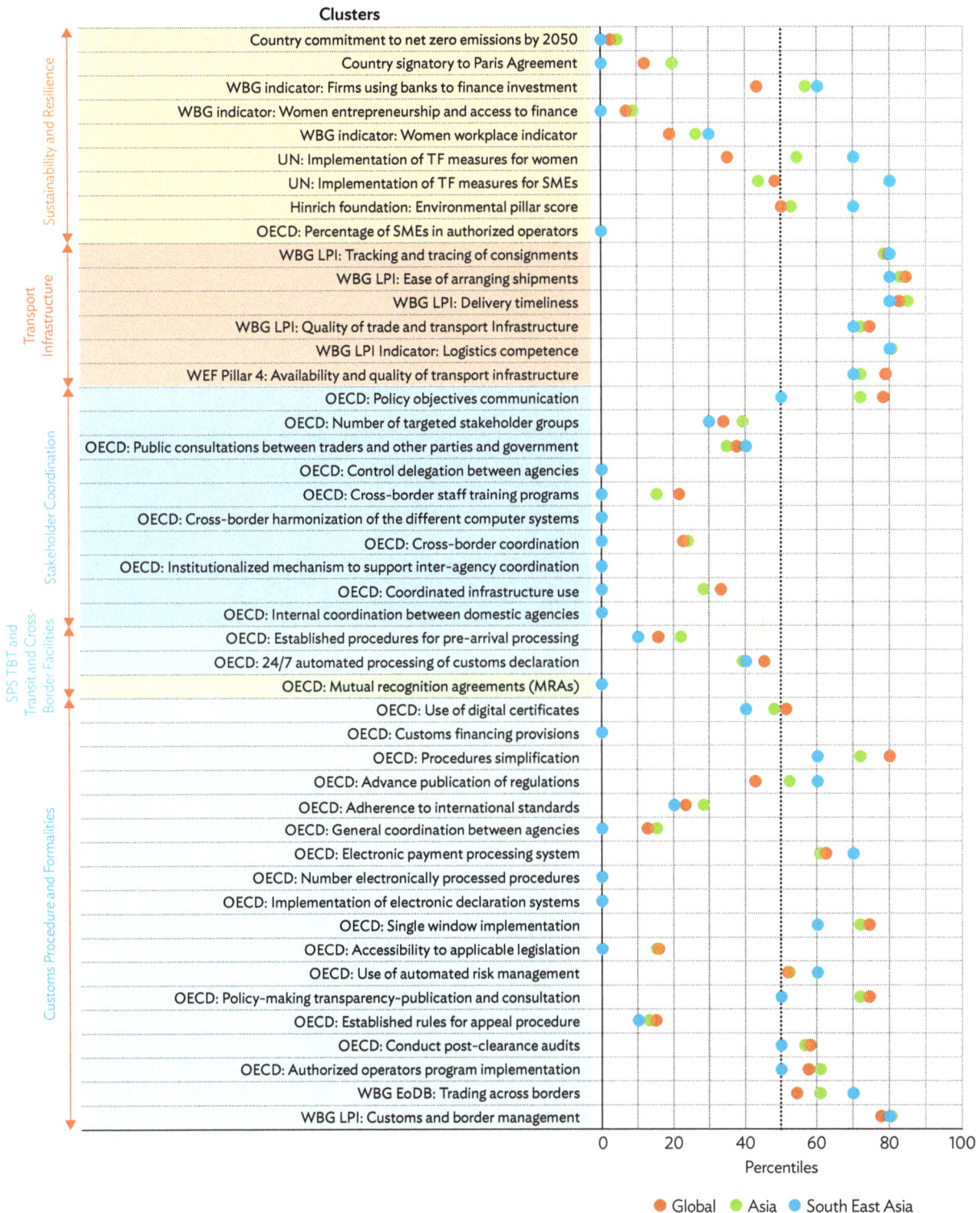

EoDB = Ease of Doing Business, OECD = Organisation for Economic Co-operation and Development, SMEs = small and medium-sized enterprise, TF = trade facilitation, UN = United Nations, WBG LPI = World Bank Group Logistics Performance Index, WEF = World Economic Forum.

Sources: Reports published on respective indices (details in Appendix 3), study team's estimates.

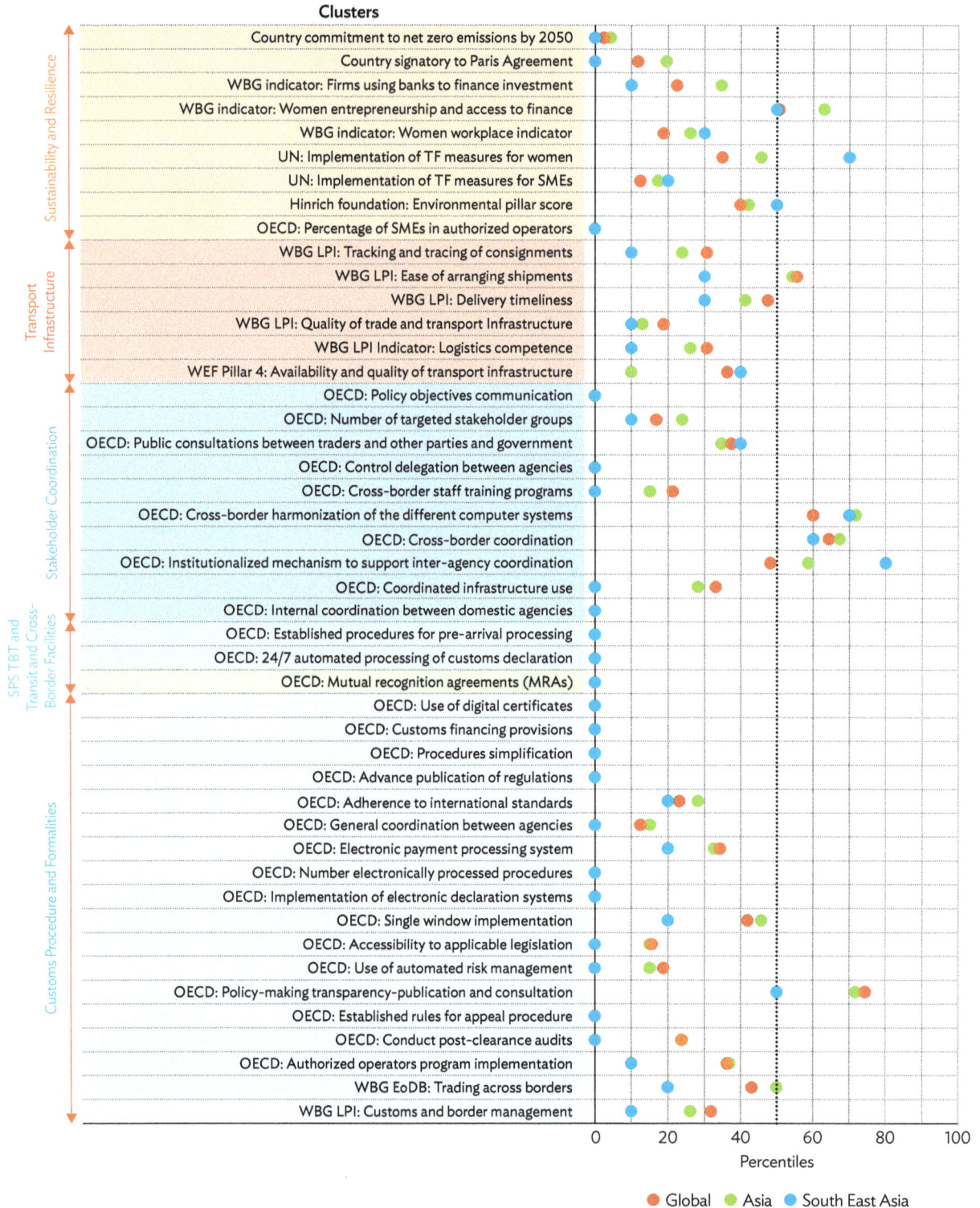

Figure 14: Position of Cambodia
(%)

EoDB = Ease of Doing Business, OECD = Organisation for Economic Co-operation and Development, SMEs = small and medium-sized enterprise, TF = trade facilitation, UN = United Nations, WBG LPI = World Bank Group Logistics Performance Index, WEF = World Economic Forum.

Sources: Reports published on respective indices (details in Appendix 3), study team's estimates.

Table 26 details indicators for which Thailand and Cambodia score below the 50th percentile, relative to global, Asian, and Southeast Asian samples, by keeping a threshold of 50%. The scores of Cambodia are comparatively lower than those of Thailand.

Measuring subnational readiness

Similar to measuring national readiness, a sample assessment of subnational readiness is conducted for the Southern Economic Corridor consisting of border-crossing points between Bangkok and Phnom Penh through secondary research. Each indicator is provided in context obtained from desk research from reports, publications, customs websites, independent studies, time release studies, etc., for benchmarking.

The Aranyaprathet and Poipet border points have been benchmarked against the researched contextual scenarios for 43 indicators across the six clusters as per the subnational readiness framework developed in section 4.3. The indicators for which the border-crossing points (BCPs) perform well above comparator are highlighted in green and the ones not up to comparator in orange. Indicators not applicable to the case in study are marked in gray. Table 27 details the sample study along with the inference.

Key Inferences from the table:

- For custom procedures and formalities and stakeholders coordination clusters, Aranyaprathet BCP on the Thailand side performs better across indicators than Poipet BCP on the Cambodia side, which is indicated in the five green cells out of 12 indicators in the former, and two green cells in the latter.
- For the clusters of transit and cross-border facilities and SPS TBT, Poipet performs better across indicators, as indicated by the 10 green cells out of 12 indicators; Aranyaprathet has six indicators across which it is above comparator.
- For the clusters of Transport Infrastructure and Sustainability and Resilience, Aranyaprathet has three areas of above average performance out of 19 indicators, whereas Poipet is marked by only one green cell.
- Appendix 4 details information about the BCPs across the 43 indicators.

Table 26: List of Indicators for Which Cambodia and Thailand Lag Compared to Peers

Indicator	Cambodia			Thailand		
	Global	Asian	SE Asian	Global	Asian	SE Asian
Customs Procedures and Formalities Cluster						
OECD G11: Use of digital certificates						
OECD K8: Customs financing provisions						
OECD H34: Procedures simplification						
OECD A9: Advance publication of regulations						
OECD F4: Adherence to international standards						
OECD I1: General coordination between agencies						
OECD G6: Electronic payment processing system						
OECD G3: % of electronically processed procedures						
OECD G2: Implementation of electronic declaration system						
OECD G8: Single window implementation						
OECD A16: Accessibility to applicable legislation						
OECD G7: Use of automated risk management						
OECD A21: Policy-making transparency						
OECD D1: Established rules for appeal procedure						
OECD H16: Conduct post-clearance audits						
OECD F20: Authorized operators program implementation						
WBG Ease of Doing Business: Trading across borders						
WBG LPI indicator on customs and border management						
SPS TBT Cluster						
OECD Indicator J10: Mutual recognition agreements						
Transit and Cross-Border Facilities Cluster						
OECD Indicator H4: Established procedures for pre-arrival processing						
OECD Indicator G12: 24/7 automated processing of customs declaration						
Stakeholder Coordination Cluster						
OECD Indicator B8: Policy objectives communication						
OECD Indicator B4: Number of targeted stakeholder groups						
OECD Indicator B1: Public consultations between traders and other parties and government						
OECD Indicator I8: Control delegation between agencies						
OECD Indicator J11: Cross-border staff training programs						
OECD Indicator J5: Cross-border harmonization of the different computer systems						

continued on next page

Table 26 *continued*

Indicator	Cambodia			Thailand		
	Global	Asian	SE Asian	Global	Asian	SE Asian
OECD Indicator J1: Cross-border coordination				●		
OECD Indicator I2: Institutionalized mechanism to support inter-agency coordination	●			●		
OECD Indicator I11: Coordinated Infrastructure use	●			●	●	●
OECD Indicator I10: Internal coordination between domestic agencies	●			●	●	●
Transport Infrastructure Cluster						
WBG LPI: Tracking and tracing of consignments	●			●		
WBG LPI: On ease of arranging shipments			●	●		
WBG LPI: On delivery timeliness	●					
WBG LPI: On quality of trade and transport infrastructure	●					
WBG LPI Indicator: Logistics competence	●					
WEF Pillar 4: Availability and quality of transport infra	●		●			●
Sustainability and Resilience						
Country commitment to net zero emissions by 2050						
Country signatory to Paris Agreement						
WBG: Firms using banks to finance investment (%)	●					
WBG: Women entrepreneurship and access to finance					●	
WBG: Women workplace indicator	●		●	●	●	●
UN Survey: Trade finance measures implemented for women	●		●	●		
UN Survey: Implementation of trade finance measures for SMEs	●	●		●		
Hinrich's Sustainable Trade Index: Environment	●				●	
OECD H23: Percentage of SMEs in authorized operators	●			●		●

OECD = Organisation for Economic Co-operation and Development, SMEs = small and medium-sized enterprise, UN = United Nations, WBG LPI = World Bank group Logistics Performance Index, WEF = World Economic Forum.

Sources: Reports published on respective indices (details in Appendix 3), study team's estimate.

Table 27: Subnational Readiness Assessment for Bangkok and Phnom Penh Border-Crossing Points

Parameters	Information Requirement for Evaluation	Aranyaprathet	Poipet	Comparators
Customs Procedures and Formalities and Stakeholder Coordination				
Customs Clearance Process	Average time taken for import clearance			Average import clearance time is 2 hours 12 minutes in Thailand (Aranyaprathet)
	Percent of import declarations cleared electronically			Presence of 100% electronic clearance of import documents
	Average time taken for export clearance			Average export clearance time is 3 hours 52 minutes in the Lao PDR
	Percent of export declarations cleared electronically			Presence of 100% electronic clearance of export documents
	Rate of duplication of bureaucratic activities			Presence of electronic data exchange system and single window mechanism to eliminate duplication
	Border clearance cost			Average border import clearance cost for ASEAN as per trading-across-border indicators—$105.3
	Provision of digital payments			Presence of operational e-payment system of tariffs and duties
Pre-shipment Inspection	Time taken for pre-shipment physical inspection			Time for physical inspection should not exceed 1 day (country average as per WBG LPI)
	Percentage of physical inspection			Physical inspection should not exceed more than 5% (probability by WBG trading across borders)
Solicitation of Informal Payments	Prevalence of informal payments for cargo clearance/checkpoints/weighbridge stations/traffic stops, etc.			Transparent and digital procedures to ensure 0% informal payments
Cross-Border Coordination	Synchronization of border timings, clearance procedures			Border time harmonization requirement for seamless cargo transit across borders
	Presence of international agreements and memorandum of understanding			Presence of CBTA/MOUs/agreements to allow ease of clearance process and allow 100% of vehicles for cross-border transportation

continued on next page

Table 27 continued

Transit and Cross-Border Facilities and SPS/TBT

Parameters	Information Requirement for Evaluation	Aranyaprathet	Poipet	Comparators
Warehousing/ Transloading Facilities	Total number of warehousing facilities			Presence of at least one warehousing facility in the border-crossing point's (BCP) vicinity for ease of storage and shipments
	Presence of transshipment yard			Presence of at least one transshipment facility for loading and unloading of cargos
	Cost of warehousing and transloading			Average warehousing cost in the People's Republic of China (PRC) is $6.35 per square meter
	Compulsory warehousing/transloading process			Warehousing/transloading facilities not to be compulsory by implementing CBTA/Bilateral trade and transport agreements
Telecommunications and IT	Presence of ICT infrastructure			Presence of ICT infrastructure
	Quality of internet and mobile connectivity			Presence of secure network services with adequate bandwidth
Export Processing Zones	Presence of SEZs			Presence of Cross-Border SEZs: PRC has SEZs at the border point with Myanmar at Ruili-Muse (Myanmar) BCPs
	Presence of custom bonded warehouses			Presence of custom bonded warehousing facilities
Quality/Standards Inspection Agencies	Presence of inspection facilities			Presence of inspection facilities
	Operation of risk management system			Presence of IT tool to conduct 100% risk management system
Health/SPS Agencies	Presence of quarantine facilities			Presence of quarantine facilities
Other Facilities				X-ray for freight trucks, weighbridges, video surveillance system, radiation detectors, banks, fuelling stations, etc.

continued on next page

Table 27 *continued*

Parameters	Information Requirement for Evaluation	Aranyaprathet	Poipet	Comparators
Transport Infrastructure and Sustainability and Resilience				
Maritime Transport	Fees charged by port			Lowest demurrage and detention charges at Busan—$114
	Annual capacity			Shanghai port (world's busiest port) has an annual handling capacity of 43.3 million TEUs
	Total no. of available terminals			Shanghai port has seven terminals
	Total no. of available berths			Shanghai port has 43 berths
	Utilization percentage			70% capacity utilization is considered to be optimum as per secondary sources
	Size of containers handled			Shanghai port has the capacity to deliver 24,000 TEU container ship (largest container ship in the world)
Airport	Airport charges for cargo transit			Singapore airport import-handling service: 5% of the weight and valuation charge subject to a minimum charge of $15 per airwaybill (applicable to all charges collect shipments into Singapore)
	Time taken for cargo processing			Customs clearance time for air shipments: 3–5 days in Hong Kong, China (world's biggest cargo airport)
Road	Connectivity of a BCP to a national highway/carriageway/expressway	(green)	(green)	Connectivity to national highways/expressways
	Type of laning of the connecting road (two-laned or four-laned)		(orange)	Minimum requirement of 4 laning road for seamless cargo transport
	Availability of parking area		(orange)	Presence of adequate parking areas to avoid delays
	No. of cargo trucks exchanged per day		(orange)	Traffic volumes at the border of Ruili and Muse amount to 1,000–1,500 trucks per day
	Cost of road transport			Average road freight hauling rates in the PRC at $0.86 per kilometer
	Average time taken for cross-border cargo transport		(orange)	Moc Bai and Bavet BCP average border cargo transport time is between 1–2 hours; average outbound time at US border crossings is 14.2 minutes; and inbound time is 26.8 minutes

continued on next page

Table 27 continued

Parameters	Information Requirement for Evaluation	Aranyaprathet	Poipet	Comparators
Rail	Presence of operational rail line and haul infrastructure			Presence of operational cross-border rail line
	Cross-border synchronization of rail gauge			Presence of synchronized rail gauge on both sides of the border-crossing points
				Standard track gauge of 1,435 millimeters (mm) (4 feet, 8.5 inches) is prevalent in 60% of the global countries including parts of the PRC; 1,000 mm track gauge is largely prevalent in Cambodia, the PRC, Malaysia, Myanmar, the Lao PDR, Thailand, and Viet Nam
	Rail transport rates			Average rail freight rates at $17.43/ton–1,000 kilometers (km) in the Russian Federation (highest goods transported in railways in million tons/km as per World Bank open data)
Freight Forwarders/ Logistics Service	Charges by freight forwarders			Depends on type of goods carried and type of container (freight-forwarding charges range between $75 and $200 in the PRC)
	Type of trucks/cargo vehicles used (use of environment-friendly vehicles)			Use of environment-friendly vehicle will enable sustainable trade facilitation

Above comparator , Below comparator , Not available/not applicable .

ASEAN = Association of Southeast Asian Nations, CBTA = Cross-Border Transport Facilitation Agreement, ICT = information and communication technology, Lao PDR = Lao People's Democratic Republic, MOU = memorandum of understanding, SEZ = special economic zone, SPS/TBT = sanitary and phytosanitary technical barriers to trade, TEU = twenty-foot equivalent unit, WBG LPI = World Bank group Logistics Performance Index.

Sources: World Bank's Logistics Performance Index. https://lpi.worldbank.org/; World Bank Group. 2014. Cambodia Trade Corridor Performance Assessment. https://openknowledge.worldbank.org/handle/10986/20763; ADB. 2018. Leveraging Mongolia's Transport and Logistics Sector. Manila. https://www.adb.org/sites/default/files/publication/464891/mongolia-transport-logistics-sector.pdf; Mekong Institute. 2019. Study on Customs Modernization in the Lanchang-Mekong Countries. https://www.mekonginstitute.org/uploads/tx_ffpublication/9._Study_on_Customs_Modernization_in_the_Lancang-Mekong_Countries.pdf; Secretariat of the Trade Facilitation Committee and Lao PDR Competitiveness and Trade Project. 2020. Final Report on Time Release Study. http://www.laotradeportal.gov.la/kcfinder/upload/files/Pub_1629095799.pdf; Japan International Cooperation Agency. 2016. The Data Collection Survey on International Logistics Function Strengthening in the Kingdom of Cambodia: Final Report. Tokyo. https://openjicareport.jica.go.jp/710/710_109_12284980.html

Policy Recommendations

Based on the findings of the illustrative case study and gap identification undertaken in the previous section, key indicative policy recommendations aimed at addressing the identified gaps and/or issues are detailed in this section in Tables 28 and 29. The study identifies illustrative policy recommendations for enhancing trade and transport facilitation in the section of Southern Economic Corridor in Thailand and Cambodia, analyzed as a case study.

Illustrative policy recommendations have been provided for Cambodia and Thailand, covering mostly soft interventions, and for Aranyaprathet and Poipet, that consists of a mix of hard and soft interventions. The issues have been consolidated for areas where either of the countries or BCPs fall below average or lower than 50th percentile. While the indicators for which either country is already above comparator or more than 50th percentile have not been specifically evaluated, even these cases may have scope for improvement.[11]

The references for indicative policy recommendations have been taken from verified prior studies on trade routes between Bangladesh, India, and Nepal, and from reports obtained from secondary research such as UNESCAP report *Making the WTO Trade Facilitation Agreement Work for SMEs*, UNCTAD policy briefs, UN Economic Commission for Europe Trade Facilitation Implementation Guide articles, etc.

National-Level Illustrative Policy Recommendations for Cambodia and Thailand

Table 28: National-Level Illustrative Policy Recommendations

Sl. No.	Identified Issue	Illustrative Recommendations	
		Cambodia	Thailand
Key Recommendations on Customs Procedures and Formalities			
1	Low filing of digital certificates due to lack of proper implementation of electronic declaration system and electronic processed procedures	➲ Fiscal and nonfiscal incentives to encourage digital filing of certificates by the traders to reduce dwelling time for cargo at the trading gateways ➲ Operationalization and implementation of advanced electronic declaration system to promote paperless transactions and electronic procedures	
2	Lack of adequate financing provision	➲ Provision for funding schemes, particularly for small and medium-sized enterprises and women traders ➲ Conduct workshops and awareness-training sessions to disseminate information on the custom financing provision	
3	Low adherence to international standards	➲ National-level policy provisions in line with international trade process standards to improve level of compliance	

continued on next page

---

[11] Indicators where both countries have scored more than the 50th percentile or have performance above the comparator have not been included for recommendations.

Table 28 *continued*

Sl. No.	Identified Issue	Illustrative Recommendations	
		Cambodia	Thailand
4	Lack of proper provisions for advance publication of regulations	➡ Provisions for mandatory notification system on any changes in trade regulations and process by the National Bank of Cambodia, Ministry of Commerce	* (Please see end note of the table for this reference)
5	Limited implementation of the Automated Risk Management System (consignments identified as Red Lane by ASYCUDA are manually entered into the system by frontline customs officials so that Risk Management Unit officials can assess the detailed risks further)	➡ Upgrade Customs Risk Management Database System (CRMDS 2011) to ensure objectivity in facilitation and enforcement, and expedite release of low-risk cargo ➡ Implementation of CRMDS in all of the border checkpoints in Cambodia (currently implemented in 10 main checkpoints)	*
6	Electronic payment processing system	➡ Mechanism to implement digital payment interface (e-payment module) for trade related payments in Cambodia	*
7	Lack of single window implementation	➡ Implement and upgrade the Cambodia National Single Window System, integrated with all concerned regulatory agencies providing clearances/approvals to the traders	*
8	Lack of proper rules on appeal procedures and lack of accessibility to applicable legislation	➡ Introduce initiative for a simplified appeal procedure with provisions of time periods of the procedures. ➡ Provide information on available legislation to SMEs and women traders through advance publications/SMS services, etc.	
9	Outdated manual for post clearance audits	➡ Development of up-to-date dedicated manual for post-clearance audit to create an environment of increased compliance and enhance facilitation of importers and exporters (current manual is of the year 2008)	*
10	Limited implementation for authorized economic operators	➡ Upgrade the existing Best Trader Incentive Mechanism for complete implementation as per 2023 strategy for customs reforms and modernization ➡ Introduce policy provisions for trade and regulation to facilitate special MSME Authorized Economic Operators accreditation (that require less stringent criteria) for the benefit of compliant trade	*
Key Recommendations on SPS/TBT			
11	Absence of required mutual recognition agreements (SPS standards for certain agricultural products are applied arbitrarily and without prior notification in Thailand)	➡ Initiate dialogues for mutual recognition agreements with major trading partners to recognize each other's competent conformity assessment bodies thereby reducing nontariff barriers ➡ Development of appropriate country-level legislation for the signing of mutual recognition agreements	

continued on next page

Table 28 *continued*

Sl. No.	Identified Issue	Illustrative Recommendations	
		Cambodia	Thailand
Key Recommendations on Transit and Cross-Border Facilities			
12	Low rates of pre-arrival processing	➡ Encourage traders through workshops to undertake pre-shipment testing for all consignments to avoid lag at border-crossing and for advance filling of documents to reduce dwell time of cargo at the BCP ➡ Include a provision in the country-level Customs Act to allow customs clearance of containerized export cargo at factory premises/off-border clearances prior to its movement to the respective BCPs	
		➡ Simplification of the existing advance ruling procedures in Cambodia	➡ Increase the rate of pre-arrival processing at land ports in Thailand through advanced electronic manifests and advance payment of duties and taxes by sensitization of importers and exporters on the processes
Key Recommendations on Stakeholder Consultation			
13	Limited consultations between stakeholders and internal coordination of domestic border agencies and lack of effective control delegation and institutionalized mechanism to improve interagency coordination	➡ Policy upgradation for strengthening and institutionalizing National Trade Facilitation Committee (NTFC) to represent exhaustive range of internal stakeholders have a role in trade and transport (including SMEs, women, and private sector) ➡ Conduct annual policy dialogues to improve collaboration between at-the-border and behind-the-border agencies and the private sector ➡ Set short-term and long-term goals for NTFCs to achieve 100% interagency coordination within a time frame	
14	Lack of cross-border harmonization, coordination, and infrastructure use	➡ Increase cross-border coordination through establishment of memorandum of understanding, initiatives on joint infrastructure projects, and cross-border agreements by initiating discussion with concerned authorities of the member countries ➡ Mutually share and accept weighment slips, accompanied by weighment of select import cargo (subject to risk parameters) ➡ Development of regional single window system to enable exchange of key documents between Cambodia and Thailand to further expedite cargo clearance process and reduce paperwork	
15	Automated processing of customs declaration not operational 24/7	➡ Initiate discussions with concerned authorities in Cambodia and Thailand to ensure adherence to 24/7 operations at all BCPs	
16	Lack of provisions for cross-border staff training program	➡ Develop and implement policy mandates for joint staff training programs of Thailand and Cambodia to enhance collaboration and information exchange of cross-border processes between the countries	
Key Recommendations on Transport Infrastructure			
17	Absence of tracking and tracing of consignments	➡ To ensure better monitoring of the movement of import/export cargo vehicles along the transit route and take immediate measures, in the event of any deviation/tampering of such vehicles, it is suggested to explore installation of e-seal on the Cambodia registered vehicles subject to evaluation of its commercial viability ➡ Explore deployment of a tracking system to facilitate cargo reconciliation	*

continued on next page

Table 28 *continued*

Sl. No.	Identified Issue	Illustrative Recommendations	
		Cambodia	Thailand
18	Lack of quality trade and transport infrastructure at the border	➜ Develop detailed report to undertake construction related activities to augment existing facilities and to create new facilities for trade and transport, e.g., augmentation of internal roads, parking chassis, cold storage facilities, etc.	*
Key Recommendations on Sustainability and Resilience			
19	Lack of efficient trade facilitation measures for women	➜ Implement gender-responsive trade facilitation policy measures and digital tools (promoting contactless trade) to eliminate gender-based barriers (time constraints, costs of burdensome procedures, discrimination, and harassment) at borders ➜ Build gender-sensitive NTFCs through training sessions ➜ Provision for conducting information sessions (through NTFC/other committees/bodies) for informal women traders to provide fact-based insights, and to promote women entrepreneurs in the trade and transport sector ➜ Adopt a client service charter with a code of conduct for public agents, stating the responsibilities and obligations of administrations toward women traders. Such charters should embody awareness and protection of women's rights, contributing to achieving the Sustainable Development Goals and the declaration on gender equality and diversity in customs of the World Customs Organization, as well as principles of good governance and integrity in customs ➜ Provision for favorable tax regime and trade facilitation schemes for women and informal traders ➜ Construction activities for appropriate gender-sensitive at-the-border facilities (sanitation facilities such as restroom, bathroom, accommodation, etc.) ➜ Establishment of complaint mechanism (grievance redressal mechanism) for victims of gender-based discrimination at borders.	
20	Lack of efficient Trade Environment for SMEs	➜ Provision for deferred tax/subsidized tax and duties for SMEs for expedited shipments ➜ Application of targeted compliance management approach (under risk management system) for operators that are SMEs, that favors efforts to assist them to comply rather than to penalize them for noncompliance. ➜ Trade procedures information dissemination to SMEs through regular online publication/mobile service, etc. ➜ Provision for technical consultation and training services to SMEs on registering and using the single-window facility	

ASYCUDA = Automated System for Customs Data, BCP = border-crossing point, CBTA = Cross-Border Transport Agreement, MOU = memorandum of understanding, MSME = micro, small, and medium-sized enterprise, SMEs = small and medium-sized enterprises, SMS = short messaging service, SPS/TBT = sanitary and phytosanitary/technical barriers to trade.

Note: Recommendations have not been provided for areas where Thailand scores more than the 50th percentile; however, scope may remain for strengthening these indicators for the country.

Sources: United Nations Economic and Social Commission for Asia and the Pacific (UNESCAP). 2016. *Making the WTO Trade Facilitation Agreement Work for SMEs*. https://www.unescap.org/sites/default/files/MakingWTOTFAWorkforSMEs.pdf; United Nations Conference on Trade and Development (UNCTAD). 2022. Integrating a gender perspective into trade facilitation reforms. *Policy Brief. No. 98.* https://unctad.org/system/files/official-document/presspb2022d6_en.pdf; Asian Development Bank (ADB). 2021. *Strengthening Trade Along the Dhaka–Kolkata Route*. Manila. https://www.adb.org/sites/default/files/publication/755651/strengthening-trade-dhaka-kolkata-route.pdf.

Table 29: Subnational Policy Recommendations for Aranyaprathet and Poipet

Sl. No.	Identified Issue	Illustrative Recommendations	
		Aranyaprathet (Thailand)	Poipet (Cambodia)
Key Recommendations on Soft Infrastructure			
1	Existence of practice of manual submission of supporting documents for securing approvals which increases the cargo clearance time and trade costs	➡ Online submission of all documents should be encouraged to facilitate advance filing of declarations through conducting workshops for sensitization/awareness creation among the traders as well as the customs officials to encourage the practice of online submission of all documents	
2	Prevalence of process duplication at the borders	*	➡ Operationalize National Single Window System integrated with all concerned regulatory agencies providing clearances/approvals to the traders ➡ Integrate various existing systems (on either side of the border) on a common digital platform along with development of requisite regulatory framework to enable trade, transport, and commercial data to be exchanged electronically among various government agencies and other key stakeholders
3	Lack of appropriate digital tool for customs-related payments	*	➡ Design, develop, and implement digital payment interface for trade-related payments at Poipet
4	Presence of high rates of physical inspection	➡ Implementation of advanced information-technology-driven risk management system to reduce physical inspection rate and time both at Aranyaprathet and Poipet	
5	Limited truck-exchange capacity at the borders	➡ Amend the existing bilateral MOU under the CBTA to allow 100% of vehicles to cross-border ➡ Implement Motor Vehicles Agreement across Thailand and Cambodia	
6	Use of traditional fuel trucks	➡ Public policies to adopt use of sustainable e-vehicles for the purpose of trade to reduce trade-related carbon footprint ➡ Sensitization of trucking companies through workshops/sessions on the benefits of adopting environment-friendly practices ➡ Joint regulatory intervention between Cambodia and Thailand to mandate a percentage of electric vehicles for trade	
Key Recommendations on Hard Infrastructure			
7	High traffic congestion at the BCP	➡ Augmentation of the identified road stretches in number of lanes/construction of roads on a greenfield basis on both sides ➡ Construction of an additional gate within the premises to facilitate (i) movement of all cargo vehicles within the customs premises, and (ii) passenger movement only at the existing zero point	

continued on next page

Table 29 *continued*

Sl. No.	Identified Issue	Illustrative Recommendations	
		Aranyaprathet (Thailand)	**Poipet** (Cambodia)
8	Lack of warehousing and transloading facilities, parking area, etc.	→ Conduct feasibility studies and prepare detailed report to undertake construction activities for the development of intermodal transshipment facilities → Initiate discussions with the concerned agencies to expedite development of requisite infrastructure such as a warehouse, and augment parking area to accommodate 2,000 vehicles → Implementation of an online parking management system providing real-time information on availability of parking slots at the BCPs to reduce waiting time and associated costs → Develop detailed report for augmenting internal roads and set up adequate halting, as well as maintenance/repair facilities en route to the BCP on both sides, banking facility, electronic weighbridges, inspection sheds, etc., through feasibility assessment	
9	Presence of compulsory transloading at the borders	→ Upgrade the CBTA bilateral MOU to allow 100% of the vehicles for cross-border transport without transloading[a] → Simplification of process to obtain license to drive through member country → Sensitization of the trucking companies through workshops on the process of obtaining the license	
10	Absence of custom bonded warehouses	→ Initiate discussion with customs officials and conduct feasibility study to develop custom bonded warehouses at Aranyaprathet and Poipet for improving trade → Development of a dedicated "export hub" in Aranyaprathet BCP and Poipet BCP which will allow direct entry of export cargo trucks	
11	Lack of operational rail line for trade of goods	→ Develop detailed report for construction of railway infrastructure such as track, railway sidings, goods yards, import inspection zone, etc., to facilitate import of cargo traffic, from Bangkok to Phnom Penh through Aranyaprathet and Poipet and vice versa, to reduce trade and logistics cost	
12	Lack of initiatives on sustainability and inclusiveness	→ In line with recommendations on National readiness (Table 28 of the report), implementing agencies at Aranyaprathet and Poipet need to align their action plans in line with the National-level policies around SME inclusiveness, gender equity, and sustainability of trade facilitation measures	

BCP = border-crossing point, CBTA = Cross-Border Transport Agreement, MOU = memorandum of understanding, SME = small and medium-sized enterprise.

[a] The CBTA is a single comprehensive legal instrument that includes all of the nonphysical measures for cross-border land transport. Under the CBTA, vehicles, drivers, goods and passengers will be allowed to cross national borders through the Greater Mekong Subregion (GMS) road transport system. The agreement promotes the elimination of intermediary stops or transshipment, as well as promoting the reduction in the amount of time spent in crossing borders. Increasing the number of border checkpoints that are implementing the CBTA will help maximize the effectiveness of the GMS transport networks. The CBTA complements the existing physical infrastructure of the GMS countries.

Note: Recommendations have not been provided for the areas of above comparator performance; however, scope may remain for strengthening these indicators for the BCP.

Source: Asian Development Bank. 2021. *Strengthening Trade Along the Dhaka–Kolkata Route*. Manila. https://www.adb.org/sites/default/files/publication/755651/strengthening-trade-dhaka-kolkata-route.pdf.

References

Arvis, J., Y. Duval, B. Shepherd, and C. Utoktham. 2013. Trade Costs in the Developing World: 1995–2010. Washington DC: World Bank. https://openknowledge.worldbank.org/handle/10986/12182.

Arvis, J., Y. Duval, B. Shepherd, C. Utoktham, and A. Raj. 2015. Trade Costs in the Developing World: 1996–2010. World Trade Review. Cambridge University Press.

Asian Development Bank. 2015. *The Greater Mekong Subregion Transport and Trade Facilitation Action Program (TTF-AP)*. https://www.adb.org/sites/default/files/institutional-document/173415/ttfap-brochure.pdf.

____. 2016. *The GMS Beyond Borders*. Manila. https://www.adb.org/sites/default/files/institutional-document/32613/files/gms-rcsp.pdf.

____. 2018. *Leveraging Mongolia's Transport and Logistics Sector*. Manila. https://www.adb.org/sites/default/files/publication/464891/mongolia-transport-logistics-sector.pdf.

____. 2021. *2021 Trade Finance Gaps, Growth, and Jobs Survey*. https://www.adb.org/sites/default/files/publication/739286/adb-brief-192-trade-finance-gaps-jobs-survey.pdf.

Brunet-Jailly, E. 2022. *Cross-border cooperation: a global overview. Alternatives (Boulder)*. National Centre for Biotechnology Information. https://www.ncbi.nlm.nih.gov/pmc/articles/PMC8905113/.

Cullinane, K. and H. Haralambides. 2021. Global trends in maritime and port economics: the COVID-19 pandemic and beyond. *Maritime Economics & Logistics*. https://link.springer.com/article/10.1057/s41278-021-00196-5.

Egger, P., M. Larch, S. Nigai, and Y. Votov. 2021. Trade Costs in the Global Economy: Measurement, Aggregation and Decomposition. *WTO Working Paper*. https://www.wto.org/english/res_e/reser_e/ersd202102_e.htm.

GIZ. n.d. Partnership Ready Rwanda: Transport. https://www.giz.de/en/downloads/giz2021_en_Partnership_Ready_Rwanda_Transport.pdf.

Gonzales, J. L. and S. Sorescu. 2019. *Helping SMEs Internationalize through Trade Facilitation*. OECD. https://www.oecd-ilibrary.org/trade/helping-smes-internationalise-through-trade-facilitation_2050e6b0-en.

Hummels, D. and A. Skiba. 2004. Shipping the Good Apples Out? An Empirical Confirmation of the Alchian-Allen Conjecture. *Journal of Political Economy*. 112(6). https://www.journals.uchicago.edu/doi/epdf/10.1086/422562.

Insurance Information Institute. n.d. *Facts + Statistics: Global catastrophes*. https://www.iii.org/fact-statistic/facts-statistics-global-catastrophes.

International Finance Corporation. 2020. *The Impact of COVID-19 on Logistics*. https://www.ifc.org/wps/wcm/connect/2d6ec419-41df-46c9-8b7b-96384cd36ab3/IFC-Covid19-Logistics-final_web.pdf?MOD=AJPERES&CVID=naqOED5.

International Trade Centre. 2021. *SME Competitiveness Outlook 2021: Empowering the Green Recovery*. https://intracen.org/resources/publications/sme-competitiveness-outlook-2021-empowering-the-green-recovery.

Kurmanalieva, E. 2020. Infrastructure Quality, Cross-Border connectivity and Trade Costs. *ADBI Working Paper Series* No. 1208 Tokyo: ADB Institute. https://www.adb.org/sites/default/files/publication/668346/adbi-wp1208.pdf.

Organisation for Economic Co-operation and Development. n.d. *Global value chains and trade*. n.d. https://www.oecd.org/trade/topics/global-value-chains-and-trade/.

____. 2018. *Trade Facilitation and the Global Economy*. https://www.oecd-ilibrary.org/sites/9789264277571-5-en/index.html?itemId=/content/component/9789264277571-5-en.

____. 2020. *OECD Economic Surveys: Poland 2020 - Boosting SMEs' Internationalization*. https://www.oecd-ilibrary.org/sites/d97e2c43-en/index.html?itemId=/content/component/d97e2c43-en.

Ross, L. 2020. Inside the iPhone: How Apple Sources From 43 Countries Nearly Seamlessly. *Thomas Insights*. https://www.thomasnet.com/insights/iphone-supply-chain/.

Rubinova, S. and M. Sebti. 2021. *The WTO Trade Cost Index and its Determinants*. WTO. https://www.wto.org/english/res_e/reser_e/ersd202106_e.pdf.

Srivastava, P. and U. Kumar, eds. 2012. *Trade and Trade Facilitation in the Greater Mekong Subregion*. ADB. https://think-asia.org/handle/11540/1438.

Staples, B. R. and J. Harris. 2009. Origin and Beyond: Trade Facilitation Disaster or Trade Facilitation Opportunity? *ADBI Working Paper Series* No.171. Tokyo: ADB Institute. https://www.adb.org/sites/default/files/publication/156026/adbi-wp171.pdf.

United Nations Conference on Trade and Development (UNCTAD). 2011. *Trade Facilitation in Regional Agreements*. Geneva. https://unctad.org/system/files/official-document/dtltlb2011d1_en.pdf.

____. 2020. *Adapting the use of ASYCUDA World to the COVID-19 situation: Guidelines to customs administrations*. https://unctad.org/system/files/official-document/dtlasycudainf2020d1_en.pdf.

____. 2022a. *Impact of the COVID-19 Pandemic on Trade and Development: Lessons Learned*. https://unctad.org/system/files/official-document/osg2022d1_en.pdf.

____. 2022b. *Integrating a gender perspective into trade facilitation reforms*. https://unctad.org/system/files/official-document/presspb2022d6_en.pdf.

United Nations Economic Commission for Europe (UNECE). n.d. *Trade facilitation - principles and benefits*. https://tfig.unece.org/details.html.

UNECE and UN Centre for Trade Facilitation and Electronic Business. 2018. *Women in Trade Facilitation*. https://unece.org/fileadmin/DAM/cefact/GuidanceMaterials/WhitePapers/WP_Women-TF_Eng.pdf.

United Nations Economic and Social Commission for Asia and the Pacific (UNESCAP). 2021. *Digital and Sustainable Trade Facilitation: Global Report 2021*. https://www.unescap.org/sites/default/d8files/knowledge-products/UNTF-Global%20Report-web%2B.pdf.

____. 2021. *Trade facilitation in times of crisis and pandemic*. Retrieved from https://www.unescap.org/sites/default/d8files/knowledge-products/Regional%20report-Trade%20facilitation%20in%20times%20of%20crisis%20and%20pandemic_0.pdf.

UNESCAP and UNCTAD. 2019. *The Asia-Pacific Trade and Investment Report 2019: Navigating Non-tariff Measures towards Sustainable Development*. United Nations. https://www.unescap.org/publications/APTIR2019.

____. 2021. *Asia-Pacific Trade and Investment Report 2021: Accelerating Climate-smart Trade and Investment for Sustainable Development*. United Nations. https://www.unescap.org/sites/default/d8files/knowledge-products/APTIR2021_3.pdf.

Vidya, C. T. and F. Taghizadeh-Hesary. 2020. Does Infrastructure Facilitate Trade Connectivity? Evidence from ASEAN. *ADBI Working Paper Series* No. 1179. Tokyo: ADB Institute. https://www.adb.org/sites/default/files/publication/634756/adbi-wp1179.pdf.

Wilson, J. S., C.L. Mann, and T. Otsuki. 2003. Trade Facilitation and Economic Development : New Approach to Quantifying the Impact. *World Bank Economic Review*. https://openknowledge. worldbank.org/handle/10986/17183.

World Bank Group. 2014. *Cambodia Trade Corridor Performance Assessment*. World Bank. https://openknowledge.worldbank.org/handle/10986/20763.

World Customs Organization (WCO). 2015. *Case Study National Committee on Trade Facilitation (NCTF)*. Canada: WCO. http://www.wcoomd.org/-/media/wco/public/global/pdf/topics/wto-atf/ national-committees-on-trade-facilitation/case-study-on-nctf-canada_final_2.pdf.

World Trade Organization. n.d. *WTO Trade Cost Index*. http://tradecosts.wto.org/.

———. n.d. *Trade Facilitation*. http://gtad.wto.org/trta_subcategory.aspx?cat=33121.

———. n.d. *Trade facilitation—Cutting "red tape" at the border*. https://www.wto.org/english/tratop_e/ tradfa_e/tradfa_introduction_e.htm.

———. 2020. *World Trade Report 2020*. https://www.wto.org/english/res_e/booksp_e/ wtr20_e/wtr20_e.pdf.

———. 2021a. *Trade and Climate Change Information brief No. 3*. https://www.wto.org/english/news_e/ news21_e/clim_03nov21-3_e.pdf.

———. 2021b. *Trade and climate change Information Brief No. 4*. https://www.wto.org/english/news_e/ news21_e/clim_03nov21-4_e.pdf.

———. 2022. *Trade Facilitation Agreement Database*. Accessed 29 August 2022. https://tfadatabase. org/trade-facilitation-committee/experience-sharing/topic/art-23-2-national-committee-on-trade-facilitation.

Xu, A. 2019. *Natural Disasters*. Geneva: WTO. https://www.wto.org/english/tratop_e/devel_e/ sympnaturaldisaster29112019_ankai_xu.pdf.

www.ingramcontent.com/pod-product-compliance
Lightning Source LLC
Chambersburg PA
CBHW050048220326
41599CB00045B/7322